NEW VISTAS

4

STUDENT BOOK

H. DOUGLAS BROWN

ANNE ALBARELLI-SIEGFRIED

ALICE SAVAGE

MASOUD SHAFIEI

North Harris Montgomery Community College

Internet Activities by Howard Beckerman

Heartworks International, Inc., Stony Brook, New York

Longman

Pearson Education, 10 Bank Street, White Plains, NY 10606

Vice president, director of publishing: *Allen Ascher*
Project manager: *Margaret Grant*
Vice president, director of design and production: *Rhea Banker*
Associate director of electronic production: *Aliza Greenblatt*
Executive managing editor: *Linda Moser*
Production manager: *Ray Keating*
Production editor: *Martin Yu*
Digital layout specialist: *Lisa Ghiozzi*
Director of manufacturing: *Patrice Fraccio*
Senior manufacturing buyer: *Dave Dickey*
Art director: *Patricia Wosczyk*
Cover design: *Carmine Vecchio*
Text design: *Eric Dawson, Steven Greydanus*
Illustrators: *Carlotta Tormey, Anna Veltfort, Andrew Lange, Catherine Doyle Sullivan*
Realia: *Lisa Ghiozzi, Wendy Wolf, Electra Graphics*

Photo Credits: page 16, John Warden/Stone; page 85, Lion Country Safari, Lion Country Safari, Inc. Fla; page 85, St. Augustine, St. Augustine, Ponte Vedra & The Beaches Visitors & Convention Bureau

Reviewers: Peggy Armstrong, *Kaplan Educational Services*; Leslie Biaggi, *Miami-Dade Community College*; Melanie Blair, *Catholic University of Korea*; Susan Vinsinges Caesar, *Korea University*; Ulysses D'Aquila, *City College of San Francisco*; M. Sadiq Durrani, *BNC Santa Cruz*; Sally Gearhardt, *Consultant, Santa Rosa, California*; Margot Gramer, *Consultant, New York*; Kathy Hamilton, *Elk Grove Adult Education*; Peter Jarvis, *New York City Board of Education*; Kevin Keating, *University of Arizona*; Alberto Lima, *Yazigi Language Schools, Brazil*; Margaret Masterson, *Bethune Middle School*; JoAnn Miller, *Universidad del Valle de Mexico*; Joanne Mooney, *University of Pennsylvania*; Janet K. Orr, *Shanghai Centre, Beijing*; Cheryl Pearson, *University of Houston*; Randy Schaefer, *Freelance Instructor, Japan*; Tammy Smith-Firestone, *Edgewood Language Institute*; Amporn Srisermbhok, *Srinakharinwinot University, Thailand*; M. Rita Vieira, *Yazigi Language Schools, Brazil*

Library of Congress Cataloging–in–Publication Data
Brown, H. Douglas
    New vistas, Student book 4 / H. Douglas Brown.
        p.   cm.
      ISBN 0–13–908310–3
      1. English language– – Textbooks for foreign speakers.   I. Title.
    PE1128.B7248   2001
    428.2'4--dc21   98-14842
                                         CIP

ISBN 0-13-908310-3

2 3 4 5 6 7 8 9 10—CRK—05 04 03 02

Contents

Unit	Topics	Functions
	Moving On to the World of Work Starting a new job; preparing for a presentation; e-mail; staying in touch with school friends; working in another culture; the Internet	Talking about the future; asking for and giving advice; offering help; giving written advice; interpreting a schedule; making appointments; making distinctions; discussing cross-cultural experiences; requesting and clarifying information
	Workplaces across Cultures Discussing corporate culture, benefits, loyalty to the company; résumé writing; retirement	Requesting information; giving job-related information; talking about everyday activities; talking about habits; describing the manner in which an action occurs; discuss, read, and write about frequency of action; describing future events
	Test Anxiety Investigating how to apply to universities and colleges in the U.S.; preparing for a test; writing a college-application letter; discussing entrance exams	Asking for and giving information; talking about past experiences; determining the sequence of past events; stating a purpose or reason; talking about getting/having something done; talking about making decisions
	Starting a New Job Getting advice from friends and coworkers; skills and abilities; interacting with the boss; polite requests; policies and procedures; benefits; e-mail; the help desk	Describing experiences; describing abilities and skills; confirming information; making requests; accepting requests; refusing requests; talking about past events that are continuing in the present; talking about technology
	A Real Job Learning experiences on the job; the characteristics of a good boss; qualities of a good partner; problem-solving at work; predicaments at work	Describing predicaments; giving opinions; identifying people, places, and things; giving advice; suggesting alternatives; complimenting a person; drawing conclusions; emphasizing; making excuses; apologizing
	Working Overtime Working with a team; predicaments at work; work schedules; computer problems; e-mail; voice mail; search engines	Talking about conditions; asking for advice; giving advice; confirming information; making requests; responding to requests; interpreting an informational article; discussing alternatives
	Learning, Learning Technical studies; sightseeing; lifelong learning; planning a career; rehearsing for an interview; workplace synergy; planning a workshop	Talking about plans; following technical directions; stating technical information; describing likes and dislikes; talking about ambitions; talking about sequence of events; discussing quantity; describing recent experiences
	Interpersonal Relations at Work Advancement in the workplace (getting a promotion); policies and regulations; how things work in the office; communicating effectively	Talking about changes; stating rules; expressing hope; speculating about the future; drawing conclusions; expressing and responding to anger; persuading someone not to act impulsively; talking about past advisability; talking about possibilities; giving constructive criticism; responding to criticism and giving excuses
	Friendship in the Workplace Relationships at work; homesickness; worrying about family; resolving conflicts at work, at home	Speculating about future events; talking about hypothetical situations; making assumptions about the past; talking about past possibility; talking about past advisability; talking about wishes; talking about present conditions
	Reunion Visiting Spain; dating in the office; workplace etiquette; good relationships at work	Talking about having/getting something done; reporting opinions, thoughts, and feelings; reporting what other people asked or said; expressing advice; agreeing and disagreeing; complimenting

Grammmar	Communication Skills	
	LISTENING AND SPEAKING	READING AND WRITING
• *Another (one), the other (one), the others (the other ones), others (other ones)* • Repeated past action/past state: *used to* • Present tenses with future meaning • Modals	Ask for and give advice; offer help; make appointments; discuss cross-cultural experiences	Give written advice; communicate via e-mails; interpret a schedule; set up a personal journal; scan for new words; understand words from context
• Simple present vs. present continuous • Present perfect • Placement of adverbs and prepositional phrases • Adverbial clauses with future time	Discuss daily activities; listen for details; role play a job interview; listen and take notes	Understand words from context; interpret a résumé; interpret graphs; scan for specific information; write a résumé; tally the results of a survey
• Embedded questions • Past perfect • Active causative *(have, make, get)*	Listen for specific information; discuss advantages and disadvantages of applying to college online	Read for chronological order; read an online advertisement; make a timeline from a reading; write a letter of application; write a journal entry
• Phrasal verbs: separable and inseparable • Present perfect continuous • Affirmative and negative statements; information questions	Listen for specific information and take notes; make polite requests at work; listen for details; group problem-solving	Understand words from context; read a mind map; create your own mind map; reading for humor; proofreading
• Relative clauses • Relative pronouns as subjects • Relative pronouns as objects • Modals of advice or suggestions about the past • *Not only . . . but (also)*	Discuss predicaments at work; discuss qualities of a good partner; practice small talk; make apologies; role play problem-solving at work; take notes on a TV show	Understand pronoun reference; make inferences; journal writing
• *Either . . . or* • *Both . . . and* • *Neither . . . nor* • Direct and indirect objects • Comparison of nouns	Listen for details; take notes from a recorded message; interview classmates	Write down recorded messages; write e-mail messages at work; write notes on interviews; write a descriptive paragraph; interpret ads from website companies; compare ads for search engines; write an e-mail; select magazine articles of your own and skim or scan for "gist"
• Verb + direct object + infinitive • Verb + infinitive *(to + verb)*; verb + gerund *(verb + -ing)* • Verb + either infinitive or gerund • Participles in adverbial phrases • Participles in adjective clauses • Prefixes: *im-, in-, un-, ir-, anti-, is-*	Follow spoken instructions to complete a chart; conduct a survey; listen for details; teach a recipe; plan and present a workshop in class	Read for details; read travel ads; read a flow chart and write a paragraph with the information; read and write a recipe in paragraph form; read an article for details; set goals for more writing in English
• Passive voice in the future • Passive voice with modals • Modals in the past • *Hope* • Result clauses with *so . . . (that)* • Result clauses with *such a/an . . . that*	Listen for details; draw conclusions; role play making complaints	Give personal responses to a reading; make a list of school rules and policies; list characteristics of a good coworker and supervisor; read an article and take a test on interpersonal communication skills.
• Review: Conditional in real or possible situations • Conditional in hypothetical situations • Conditional in unreal past situations • Modals in the progressive • Modals in the past • *Wish* • *Unless*	Listen for details; interview classmates and record their responses; discuss how to handle conflict situations	Take a personality test; apply *dos* and *don'ts* to particular situations; set goals for doing more reading in English
• Review: Active causative • Passive causative • Noun clauses as objects • Reported speech: commands; statements	Role play a conversation; listen for details; report on Internet or library research; takes notes based on a listening	Research a topic on the Internet or in the library; write two or three paragraphs based on the research; draw conclusions based on information from a reading

To the Teacher

New Vistas is a series that features the best of what has come to be known as "communicative language teaching," including recent developments in creating interactive, learner-centered curriculum. With *New Vistas,* your students become actively involved in their own language acquisition through collaboration with you as their guide and facilitator.

The Components of *New Vistas*

Student Books

The five-level student books begin with *Getting Started.* Here, students learn basic life skills and vocabulary. Then, in the subsequent levels, students develop their competence and proficiency step by step in all four skills.

Primary features of all the *Student Books* include a storyline with multi-ethnic characters, providing students with opportunities to be personally involved in real-life contexts for learning; a carefully graded series of pronunciation modules; many opportunities for group and pair interaction; listening comprehension exercises; a new and exciting online feature that introduces students to Internet technology; a strategy-awareness section in each unit that stimulates students to reflect on their own preferred pathways to success; and end-of-unit grammar and communication skills summaries.

Teacher's Resource Manuals

For each unit, the *Teacher's Resource Manual* provides an overview of topics, functions, communication skills, and skills standards covered. This is followed by step-by-step, explicit teaching instructions; answer keys for the exercises in the *Student Books* and the *Workbooks,* tapescripts for the listening and pronunciation exercises; grammar activity masters; and placement and achievement tests.

Workbooks

These supplements provide numerous written exercises that reinforce the grammar points and structures taught in the *Student Books. Workbook* exercises are suitable for additional in-class practice or for homework.

The Audio Programs

The audiotapes provide stimulating listening and pronunciation practice that add to the authenticity of classroom pedagogy.

UNIT 1

Lesson 1

In this lesson, you will
- talk about the future.
- ask for and give advice.
- offer help.
- give written advice.
- interpret a schedule.

Moving On

🔊 **Listen and read.**

Gina: Ivan, is that you?

Ivan: Gina? What are you doing here?

Gina: I'm just picking up some supplies. I'm working as a buyer's assistant, and I run errands for her. I'm finally working in the fashion industry! Next week I go to San Francisco with my boss, and the week after that I'm helping to arrange a charity fashion show here in Riverside. How are you doing?

Ivan: Fine, . . . great, . . . a little sleepy. I'm finishing up a training course at the technical college. I'm trying to get a job as a help-desk technician.

Gina: You look a little tired. You should get more sleep.

Ivan: I can't. I have a part-time job as a security guard, and my hours are crazy. Tonight I start work at 9:00, and all this week I'm working nights until 6 A.M. Then next week after I finish my classes, I switch to days. It's a crazy schedule. I can't wait to get a better job.

Gina: Don't worry. You will. Help-desk technicians are really in demand these days. Hey, I'm not going back to work for a couple of hours. Do you have time for coffee? I haven't seen you in a while. We can catch up on our old classmates.

Ivan: Sure . . . and I'd also like to ask your advice about a presentation I'm giving in class next week.

▸Pair **Do you have a job? If so, what do you like about it? What is difficult about it? If you don't have a job, tell your partner about a job you'd like to have.**

1 What should I wear?

▶**Pair** Ivan is going to make a presentation in his class. He's asking Gina for advice. Look at the pictures and complete each dialog using Ivan's requests and Gina's answers in the boxes below.

Asking for advice	Giving advice
How can I make sure they get all the information?	Think about what makes you feel comfortable. You could ask them to introduce themselves first.
How can I avoid communication problems?	You shouldn't wear the polo shirt and jeans. You should wear the blazer and khakis.
What should I do to create a good relationship with the audience?	Invite them to ask questions.
Would you help me decide what to wear?	You can give them written handouts.

Ivan: I'm giving a presentation in my class on Saturday.

_____

Gina: _____

Ivan: Some of the other students are older, and that makes me nervous.

_____

Gina: _____

Ivan: They might not understand my English.

_____

Gina: _____

Ivan: I have a lot of material to cover.

_____

Gina: _____

▶**Group** What would be appropriate dress for a presentation in your class? Role play a discussion of what to wear for a presentation in your class.

2 What can I do to help?

Look at the language for offering help. Match each of the offers with one of the situations below.

Would you like me to show you how to use the new program?	**Would you like a hand with** that printer?
Let me help you. You may have a virus on your hard drive. I'll take a look at it.	**I'd be happy to** come over and help you set up the new computer.

Pair **Think of another way that you could offer help in each situation.**

3 My meeting begins at 3 o'clock.

My meeting **begins** at 3 o'clock.	**I'm leaving** work early to get a haircut.

Complete each sentence with an appropriate present or future tense form of the verb.

Ms. Swain: I'm having a problem opening my e-mail, Ivan. My mother _____ to visit me
(1. come)

tonight. She e-mailed me her flight number and arrival time. And I can't open the e-mail! I

think her plane _____ at around 7:00 this evening. Will you help me?
(2. get in)

Ivan: Yes, I guess so. I _____ to your part of town anyway to buy a printer. Should I come
(3. come)

to your apartment first?

Ms. Swain: No, I _____ downtown to meet a friend for lunch.
(4. go)

Ivan: So, here's the plan. First I _____ the printer. Then I _____ to your apartment
(5. buy) *(6. get)*

by 2:00. OK?

Ms. Swain: Yes, my afternoon class _____ at 3:00, so we'll have plenty of time.
(7. start)

Ivan: Great! My afternoon class _____ at 3:30, so I promise to do the job quickly.
(8. be)

4 I'm starting at 9 o'clock on Monday morning.

Pair Read Ivan's e-mail. Do you agree with his plan? Why or why not?

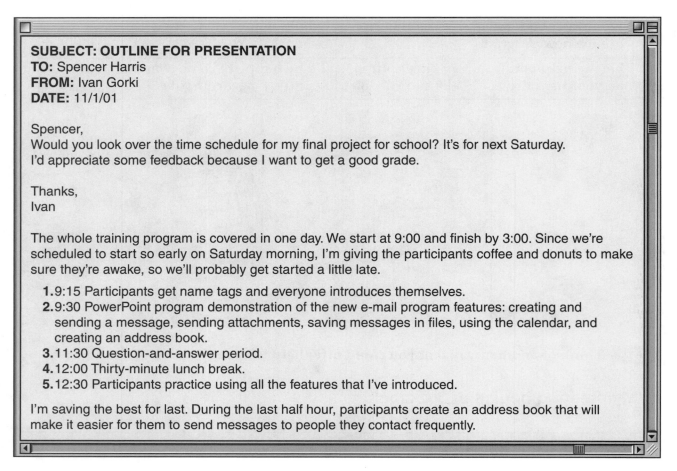

SUBJECT: OUTLINE FOR PRESENTATION
TO: Spencer Harris
FROM: Ivan Gorki
DATE: 11/1/01

Spencer,
Would you look over the time schedule for my final project for school? It's for next Saturday.
I'd appreciate some feedback because I want to get a good grade.

Thanks,
Ivan

The whole training program is covered in one day. We start at 9:00 and finish by 3:00. Since we're scheduled to start so early on Saturday morning, I'm giving the participants coffee and donuts to make sure they're awake, so we'll probably get started a little late.

1. 9:15 Participants get name tags and everyone introduces themselves.
2. 9:30 PowerPoint program demonstration of the new e-mail program features: creating and sending a message, sending attachments, saving messages in files, using the calendar, and creating an address book.
3. 11:30 Question-and-answer period.
4. 12:00 Thirty-minute lunch break.
5. 12:30 Participants practice using all the features that I've introduced.

I'm saving the best for last. During the last half hour, participants create an address book that will make it easier for them to send messages to people they contact frequently.

Pair Read Spencer's response. Then rewrite Ivan's schedule using Spencer's advice.

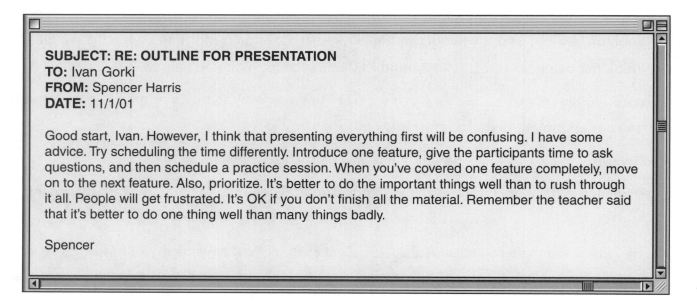

SUBJECT: RE: OUTLINE FOR PRESENTATION
TO: Ivan Gorki
FROM: Spencer Harris
DATE: 11/1/01

Good start, Ivan. However, I think that presenting everything first will be confusing. I have some advice. Try scheduling the time differently. Introduce one feature, give the participants time to ask questions, and then schedule a practice session. When you've covered one feature completely, move on to the next feature. Also, prioritize. It's better to do the important things well than to rush through it all. People will get frustrated. It's OK if you don't finish all the material. Remember the teacher said that it's better to do one thing well than many things badly.

Spencer

I'll ask him to give you a call.

Listen and read.

Ivan: I'm going to order another drink. Do you want another one?

Gina: Sure, I'll have another ginger ale. Did you say you had an e-mail from Tony?

Ivan: Yes. He works at a small factory that makes toasters.

Gina: I thought he was interested in journalism.

Ivan: Yes, but he wants to experience the life of a U.S. worker before he goes to college.

Gina: Interesting. Oh, guess what Sofia's doing.

Ivan: Working at a hospital?

Gina: Close. She's working as a paramedic right now. She wants to get more experience in the medical field before she applies to pre-med.

Ivan: That makes sense. What about Yumiko?

Gina: She went back to Japan. And . . . Lynn and I are sharing an apartment. Right now she's working for a government agency that helps immigrants find jobs. She wants to be a social worker, so she's going to college at night. By the way, have you heard from Nelson? I heard he's in the computer business.

Ivan: Yes, I talked to him the other day. He just got a job with a company that designs websites.

Gina: That's great. I may need his help. I'd like to design a website for people studying English—a place for people to share their experiences and get support. I'm sure similar websites already exist, but mine is going to be unique.

Ivan: That sounds great. I'll ask him to give you a call.

▶ **Pair** Do you have any classmates who have moved away? If they are working now, do their jobs match the goals they had when you were classmates?

1 When would be a good time for us to get together?

🎧 Gina and Nelson are talking on the phone trying to make an appointment to see each other. Listen to their conversation and complete their calendars.

	Monday	Tuesday	Wednesday	Thursday	Friday	Saturday
Gina		10 A.M. dentist appointment			4 P.M. get oil change	9:00 A.M. go to gym
Nelson	8 P.M. pick Jim up at the airport		all-day workshop	go to the bank in the afternoon	evening, go out with Ivan and Tony	

▶ Pair Do you use a calendar or planner to keep track of your plans? How often do you check your calendar or planner? Bring your planner or calendar to class and compare it with your partner's.

2 I need to make an appointment.

Read the following statements used to make appointments or plans. Then match each statement to the person with whom the appointment is being made.

1. I'd like to make an appointment for tomorrow.

2. Are we still on for dinner tomorrow evening?

3. Are you going to be in your office this afternoon? I'd like to show you my new proposal.

4. It needs to be fixed right away. What's the earliest time you can come and look at it?

5. I'd like to speak with you about my son's work. Can I come in around 3:00 on Thursday?

_____ friend

_____ boss

_____ plumber

_____ dentist

_____ teacher

▶ Pair Prepare a role-play of a phone conversation using one of the statements above. Then present your role-play to the class.

3 May I see another one?

Nelson is in a computer store. Complete the sentences with *another (one), the other (one), the others (the other ones),* or *others (other ones).*

My **scanner** doesn't work. I need **another (one)**.	This **software package** is difficult to use. Are there any **others (other ones)**?
The company has **two stores**. One is on Pine Street. **The other (one)** is on Fifth Avenue.	There are **three computers** on display. One is a Mac. **The others (the other ones)** are IBMs.

Salesclerk: How can I help you?

Nelson: My scanner doesn't work. I need

    _____.
       1

Salesclerk: We have two good, rather

    inexpensive scanners. Here's one of them.

Nelson: May I see _____?
                2

Salesclerk: Here it is. They're both $130, but you

    can get 30 percent off the price today.

Nelson: Do you have any _____? I'd
                       3

    really like something cheaper.

Salesclerk: Yes. These top-of-the-line scanners

    are on sale for $99. And here's _____
                                    4

    for only $55. It's slower than the

    _____, however.
      5

Nelson: I think the one for $55 will be fine. And

    how much are those diskettes on the shelf?

Salesclerk: The high-density ones are $5 a box.

    The _____ are $4 and $3.50.
             6

Nelson: Give me a box of the high-density ones,

    please. By the way, do you know the name of

    a store that sells computer chips?

Salesclerk: That would be Landmark. They

    have two stores. One is on Pine Street, and

    _____ is on Fifth Avenue.
         7

Nelson: Thanks. And, oh, the software package

    I bought the other day is really difficult to

    use. Are there any _____?
                        8

Salesclerk: Sorry, that's the only one of that

    kind on the market.

Nelson: Well, I guess I'll just have to get used to

    it. Thanks, anyway.

Lesson 3

In this lesson, you will

- discuss cross-cultural experiences.   • request and clarify information.

Working across Cultures

Have you ever thought about working in another country? Listen and read an article with some useful tips.

LIVING MAGAZINE
SEPTEMBER 2000

Relocation within one's own country involves changing cities, homes, schools, and offices. Moving abroad involves these changes, but in addition, this relocation includes lifestyle and cultural changes and different work ethics and attitudes.

If you have had previous experience conducting business overseas, you will certainly have a more realistic idea of what life and work will be like in your new country. Yet, there is no substitute for living there. When you actually relocate abroad, it will help if you attempt to be flexible, tolerant, and open-minded when you meet people with different cultural values.

To succeed in international business efforts, you must first understand the country's culture and manners as well as what is considered acceptable business protocol—in short, how individuals within this culture think. For example, in some countries, it is important to establish a more personal relationship, such as at a social dinner, with your business associates before you meet with them professionally. Likewise, some managers will be appalled if you begin a business transaction before the standard "getting to know you chat." In other countries, the business dealings may take precedence over social gatherings and may even replace them.

In addition, little things such as the proper presentation of business cards or addressing people only by their last names can have a tremendous impact on whether or not you will succeed in business within a particular country.

If your new assignment requires another language, you should at least have a basic knowledge of that language before you begin working in the country. After that, any sincere effort to learn the language will be highly regarded and valued by your foreign colleagues.

Source: "Relocation—Business Strategies Abroad," Insiders' Guide Online[sm]
http://www.insiders.com/relocation/18bus.htm

Pair   Do people you know generally accept people from other countries as they are? Or do they expect them to behave in the same way that they do? Discuss people you know with your partner and then tell the class about them. Give specific examples, if possible.

8   **UNIT 1**

1 Didn't the mailroom use to be here?

🎧 Tony's boss, Ms. Simms, is showing the floor plan of the newly remodeled factory to an employee who just came back from an overseas assignment. Listen to their conversation.

▶**Pair** Ask and answer questions about the location of the departments and services, using the list below as your cues. Note: The numbers in the list refer to the floor plan.

A: **Didn't** the *mailroom* **use to be** here? B: Yes, it did. But now it's the *supply room.*	A: **Didn't** *accounting* **use to be** here? B: No. *Maintenance* has always been here.

1. mailroom
2. accounting
3. director's office
4. loading dock
5. manufacturing
6. conference room
7. maintenance
8. cafeteria
9. supply room

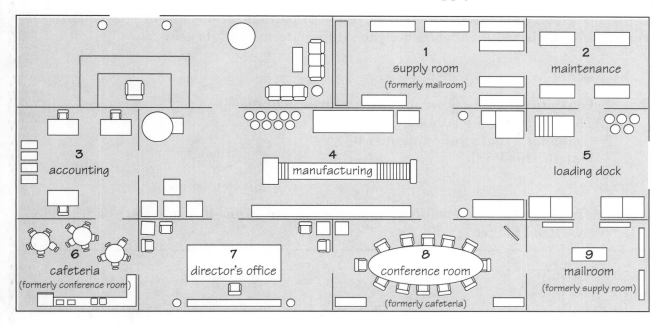

2 In Brazil, Tony used to call his bosses by their last names.

▶**Pair** Look at the ways Tony has adapted to his workplace environment. Make sentences comparing his behavior in Brazil and in the United States.

Tony **used to call** his bosses by their last names. Now he can call his boss by her first name.

In Brazil . . .	In the United States . . .
1. call boss by last name	first name
2. stand close to coworkers when talking	farther away
3. greet business associates with a hug	handshake
4. discuss business over dinner	in the office

3 What is the Internet, anyway?

Nelson is sending Gina an e-mail attachment about the Internet. Read the attachment.

The Internet is one of the most recent innovations in the field of technology. Although the idea of the Internet was conceived about forty years ago, it became popular only in the early 1990s. The Internet is a collection of millions of computers that are all linked together on a computer network. The network allows all the computers to communicate with one another. A home computer is usually linked to the Internet using a normal phone line and a modem that "talks" to an ISP (Internet Service Provider). A website is a series of pages that are created by companies or individuals and posted, or uploaded, on the Internet. Every website has an address. If you don't know a website's address, or you want to find information about a subject, you can use a search engine, such as Yahoo, Infoseek, or Excite. A search engine is simply a website that has the capability to find information on the Internet.

Some people have access to the Internet through their companies, while others pay for it themselves. The Internet is used for different purposes. While some people use it to find information, others use it to shop or trade stocks. Still other people use the Internet to send and receive e-mail.

Pair **Have you used the Internet? If so, tell your partner about some of your favorite websites. If not, discuss what you know about the Internet and its uses.**

4 Online

Log onto http://www.prenhall.com/brown_activities
The Web: Working Abroad
Grammar: What's your grammar IQ?
E-mail: This Week

5 Wrap Up

An American businessperson working in another culture wrote to a colleague back in the United States. Read the letter.

Dear Anne,

Thanks for the funny birthday card! Things are going well here, but there's something I am puzzled about. I wanted to see what you thought about it.

In the States, I always got immediate feedback from my employees, and I felt assured that they had understood what I was saying. I used to get very upset if the employee came back a day or two later and told me that he or she really hadn't understood. I always used to say, "If you didn't understand, why didn't you tell me? Why did you wait?"

Now that I'm working in another culture, I find that I need to adapt to differences in my working environment. For example, I am very uncomfortable with prolonged silence in a meeting. The other day I made a presentation at a business meeting. No one said anything when I finished, so I didn't know if they had understood me or not. I asked for questions, but no one had any. I didn't know what to do next. So I just ended the meeting. Any suggestions?

Your pal abroad,

Bill

1. Why do you think Bill used to get upset when his employees waited a day or two to tell him that they hadn't understood? Would you get upset?

2. In your culture, is silence seen as a good way to deal with problems or do people mainly depend on words to express themselves? Explain your answer.

3. Are you comfortable with silences in conversations? Or do they make you uncomfortable? What do you do when there are silences?

Strategies for Success

> ➤ **Setting personal goals**
> ➤ **Practicing giving advice**
> ➤ **Learning vocabulary through context**

1. Set up your journal for this new course. Write five major goals that you will try to accomplish during this course. (For example, "I will speak up once a day in class." "I will practice using the new vocabulary words from each unit in this book." "I will write in my journal at least once a week." "I will listen to English on TV every day." "I will read English for 15 minutes every day.")

2. Identify two or three "problems" you have (which computer to buy, what to wear somewhere, etc.). With a partner, give each other some advice about how to solve the problem. Use language that you practiced in Lesson 1.

3. The opener of Lesson 3 is an article about working in a new country. Scan the article for words you don't know (examples: *ethics, protocol*). List them. Now, with a partner, figure out their meaning from their context (topic, sentences before and after).

CHECKPOINT

How much have you learned in this unit? Review the goals for each lesson. What skills can you confidently use now? What skills do you need to practice? List these below.

Skills I've Learned Well

_____

_____

_____

_____

Skills I Need to Practice

_____

_____

_____

_____

Learning Preferences

In this unit, which type of activity did you like the best and the least? Write the number in the box: 1 = best; 2 = next best; 3 = next; 4 = least.

❑ Working by myself

❑ Working with a partner

❑ Working with a group

❑ Working as a whole class

In this unit, which exercises helped you to learn to:

listen more effectively?   Exercise _____

speak more fluently?   Exercise _____

read more easily?   Exercise _____

write more clearly?   Exercise _____

Which exercise did you like the most? _____   Why? _____

Which exercise did you like the least? _____   Why? _____

Vocabulary

Verbs	**Nouns**		**Offering Help**
create	accounting	maintenance	Would you like a
prioritize	attachment	manufacturing	hand with . . . ?
save	blazer	name tag	I'd be happy to . . .
scan	computer diskettes	scanner	Let me help you.
schedule	conference room	screen	Would you like me
	feedback	search engine	to . . . ?
	handout	software	
	khakis	supply room	
	loading dock	website	
	mailroom		

► GRAMMAR SUMMARY

Another (one), the other (one), the others (the other ones), others (other ones)

My **scanner** doesn't work. I need **another (one)**.	This **software package** is difficult to use. Are there any **others (other ones)**?
The company has **two stores**. **One** is on Pine Street. **The other (one)** is on Fifth Avenue.	There are **three computers** on display. **One** is a Mac. **The others (the other ones)** are IBMs.

Repeated past action/past state

Tony **used to call** his bosses by their last names. **Didn't** the mailroom **use to be** here?

Present tenses with future meaning

My meeting **begins** at 3 o'clock.	**I'm leaving** work early to get a haircut.

Modals

Would you **like** me to show you how to use the new program?	**Would** you **like** a hand with that printer?
Let me help you. You **may have** a virus on your hard drive.	**I'd be** happy to come and help you set it up.

► COMMUNICATION SUMMARY

Making distinctions

The company has two stores. One is on Pine Street. The other is on Fifth Avenue.

Discussing cross-cultural experiences

In Brazil, Tony used to discuss business over dinner. Now he discusses it in the office.

Asking for and giving advice

Would you help me decide what to wear?
You should wear the blazer and khakis.

Offering help

Would you like a hand with that printer?
I'd be happy to come and help you set it up.

Making appointments

I'd like to make an appointment for tomorrow.
Are we still on for dinner tomorrow evening?

Requesting and clarifying information

Didn't the mailroom use to be here?
Yes, it did. But now it's the supply room.

Giving written advice

Try scheduling the time differently. Introduce one feature, give the participants time to ask questions, and then schedule a practice session.

Talking about the future

My meeting begins at 3 o'clock.
I'm leaving work early to get a haircut.

UNIT 2

Lesson 1

In this lesson, you will
- request information.
- give job-related information.
- talk about everyday activities.
- talk about habits.

Learning the Corporate Culture

🎧 **Yumiko has a job at the Fujifilm™ lab in Japan. Her job is testing the newest color film. Listen as she reads her letter to Lynn.**

Hi, Lynn,

Guess what? I got the job at Fujifilm I was telling you about. I'm working in the film-processing lab. My title is Film Specialist, and, as a new hire, I'm in the Class F salary range. That means that the salary I'm getting now is my base pay, and, according to my present contract, I get a 5 percent increase each year over that salary level.

The company has an excellent benefits program. I'll get a bonus in the summer and in the winter. I also have 10 paid vacation or sick days a year, plus government-approved holidays—some as long as an entire week! Those long holidays are a definite perk. Don't you agree?

As a junior employee, I'm expected to organize office parties and functions like the spring flower viewing in the park. I can anticipate working long hours, and I'm never supposed to leave the office before my boss does.

All decisions are considered group decisions and they require unanimous support from all the members of our team. This slows down the process a bit, but it allows everyone to share in the reward or blame. I think it's a very good policy.

Well, tell everyone in Riverside I send my regards. Write soon.

Yumiko

▶ **Pair** How do employees in your country make agreements with each other and with their employers? Are they expected to do other tasks that are not specifically related to their job descriptions?

1 Yumiko is working in the lab.

▶**Pair** Complete the sentences with the appropriate verb forms.

> The process usually **goes** very quickly, but today it **is going** very slowly.

It's 12:00 noon and Yumiko _____ (1. work) in the lab. Normally, Yumiko
_____ (2. have) lunch before developing a new roll of film. Today, however, she
_____ (3. decide) not to have lunch first because she _____ (4. take) some
interesting shots of people and places with a brand-new color film. The developing process
usually _____ (5. go) very quickly. But today it _____ (6. go) very slowly.
Printing that normally _____ (7. take) fifteen minutes _____ (8. take) half an
hour. Something is wrong with the developing fluid. Yumiko _____ (9. get) a
headache. She _____ (10. be) very hungry, but she _____ (11. have to) continue
until she _____ (12. finish) the job.

2 Yumiko usually wears a lab coat, but today she's wearing jeans.

▶**Pair** Yumiko is taking a day off from her job at the lab. Look at each pair of pictures and
talk about Yumiko. What does she usually do? What is she doing today?

Usually	Today

▶**Group** In a small group of three or four, take turns asking each other what family members
(or close friends) usually do during the day and what they're doing today.

3 Yumiko hopes to become a team leader at Fujifilm.

Pair What qualities and skills does a leader have? Read the statements in the survey to your partner and see if he or she agrees or disagrees. Check *Yes* or *No*.

		Yes	No
1.	In a group situation, a good team leader actively invites others to take part in the discussion.	☐	☐
2.	When people in the group contribute good ideas, the team leader lets them know that their contributions are valued.	☐	☐
3.	The team leader has a clear vision of where the group or organization is headed.	☐	☐
4.	The team leader influences others to think, act, and accomplish the set goals.	☐	☐
5.	The team leader feels that differences of opinion among individuals within a work group must be resolved.	☐	☐
6.	The team leader must be in control at all times.	☐	☐

Class Do you agree with your partner? Report your answers to the class and explain why you agree or disagree.

4 Fujifilm saves the koala.

Listen to the news broadcast about one of Fujifilm's local projects. Mark the sentences True or False.

		True	False
1.	Hanimex is the name of the koala.	☐	☐
2.	The project is relocating koalas to safe places.	☐	☐
3.	The project uses radios to monitor the koalas.	☐	☐
4.	Not many people take photographs of koalas.	☐	☐
5.	TV crews follow Fuji's care program.	☐	☐

Source: http://home.fujifilm.com/news/snap11.html

5 How long have you lived here?

As part of her job application process, Yumiko had to write a résumé. Look at her résumé.

Yumiko Sato
6615 Ginza, Chuo-Ku
Tokyo, Japan
813-357-14912

Education:
1999   English language proficiency certificate, World Language Center, Riverside, CA
1998   Film-processing certificate, Riverside Community College
1997   High school diploma, Yokota High School, Tokyo, Japan

Employment:
1999–present   Film processor intern, Fujifilm Company
1999   Bank clerk, Riverside Union Bank
1997–1998   Freelance photographer, *National Geographic*; other publications

Skills:
Speak English, Spanish, and Japanese
Karate

Memberships:
1998–present   International Society of Photographic Journalists (ISPJ)
1996–1997   Honors Society, Yokota High School, Tokyo, Japan

Awards:
1997   National Honor Society, Tokyo, Japan
1996   First prize in photography competition, Tokyo, Japan

Pair   Use Yumiko's résumé and the phrases below to role play Yumiko's interview. The year is 2001. Use appropriate tenses.

1.   How long/have your film-processing certificate

2.   What kind of training/have since college

3.   How long/be a film processor

4.   How long/be a member of the ISPJ

Now write a résumé of your own. Then role play a job interview with your partner.

Lesson 2

In this lesson, you will
- discuss, read, and write about frequency of action.
- talk about habits.
- describe the manner in which actions occur.

Training to Be a Chef

🔊 Oscar is back in Spain training to be a chef in his uncle's restaurant. Listen as he explains his plans to Tony.

Oscar: Hey, Tony, how's it going?

Tony: Wow, Oscar, are you calling from Spain?

Oscar: Yeah, I'm at my uncle's restaurant. I practically live here now.

Tony: You're finally in the restaurant business. So, how's it going?

Oscar: Well, I work long hours—every night of the week—and sometimes I feel totally exhausted. But then I look out into the dining room and see people happily eating my paella or my roasted chicken. And I feel happy, too.

Tony: You talk like a true chef. Do you plan to open your own restaurant sometime?

Oscar: Oh, yeah, sure. I'm actually learning a lot here, but my uncle makes all the decisions. It's his place. He's the boss.

Tony: Well, I know you can cook beautifully, but what about the business side of it? Are you learning enough to handle the money on your own?

Oscar: Once in a while I do some ordering, but you're right, I need a lot more training in the business. And that's why I'm here! Well, I have to go now. Send me an e-mail.

Tony: Sure. Tomorrow. Take care. Bye.

Oscar: Bye.

▶ **Pair** Have you ever thought about opening a restaurant? Describe your ideal restaurant to a partner.

1 Oscar can already make a few gourmet dishes.

Use the words and phrases in the box to complete Oscar's letter to Nelson. You can use some words or phrases more than once.

Frequency	Manner	Place	Time
always never	quickly immensely financially carefully certainly easily unfortunately	here at work	yesterday next week already now soon

Dear Nelson,

I received your letter ___yesterday___ . I was so surprised to hear that your job
                         1
search went so _____ . I _____ knew you'd _____ be able to find
                   2   3   4
a job designing websites, but I _____ thought you'd get hired so _____ .
                                    5   6
So you'll be starting your new job _____ ? I've _____ heard that there's
                                      7   8
a lot of money to be made in the computer industry. If you don't mind my asking,
how will you make out _____ ? I bet you'll be making tons of money!
                         9

I'm working at my uncle's restaurant. I _____ expected to spend so
                                           10
much time _____ . I practically live _____ . _____ , the pay isn't
             11   12   13
great, but it's the job I've always wanted. I'm enjoying it _____ , and I'm
                                                                14
learning a lot. I can _____ make a few gourmet dishes. My uncle says I'm
                         15
_____ good enough to become a cook on the line. That means I get to work in
   16
the busiest and the most dangerous part of the kitchen—at the stove. You can bet
that I'll work very _____ !
                       17

I'm sorry, I think I got butter all over this letter. I'd better get it in
the mail before I get it any dirtier. It's almost time for the dinner rush. Write
_____ .
   18

Oscar

2 I frequently eat out.

Fill out the questionnaire by checking the appropriate boxes.

	Less than once a month	Once a week or less	At least twice a week	Every day
How often do you eat lunch or breakfast in a restaurant?	☐	☐	☐	☐
How often do you have dinner out with friends or family?	☐	☐	☐	☐
How often do you have dinner out for work or business?	☐	☐	☐	☐
How often do you order food to be delivered to your home or office?	☐	☐	☐	☐
How often do you have a restaurant cater your parties?	☐	☐	☐	☐

▶ **Class** Collect the questionnaires and tally the results of your survey on the board. Discuss the results.

3 How often do you eat out?

▶ **Pair** Fill in the blank with the appropriate word from the box.

never   rarely   occasionally   sometimes   often   frequently   always

1. I eat lunch in a restaurant **once a month**.

   I ___rarely___ eat lunch in a restaurant.

2. I have a business dinner **twice a week**.

   I _____ have business dinners.

3. I cook at home **every day**.

   I _____ go out to eat.

4. **Every time I have a party**, I have a restaurant cater it.

   I _____ have restaurants cater my parties.

5. I eat with friends **about five times a week**.

   I _____ eat with friends.

4 The restaurant is busiest on Saturday nights.

Listen to the conversation between Oscar and his uncle. Circle the correct answer to complete each sentence.

1. In the afternoon, customers sit   a. outside.   b. inside.

2. In the afternoon, Oscar is busiest   a. serving snacks.   b. serving dinner.

3. The restaurant serves the most meals   a. at lunch.   b. at dinner.

4. Oscar says the restaurant has more employees   a. during the day.   b. at night.

5. Oscar is excited because   a. he's making good money.   b. people like his cooking.

▶ **Pair** Describe your eating habits to your partner.

5 I'm going to start simply.

Listen to the conversation between Oscar and his father and write notes about how each person handles the situation.

Uncle Alonzo	Aunt Petra	Oscar

▶ **Group** Oscar's father is thinking about investing in Oscar's restaurant. Discuss reasons why he should or should not invest.

Lesson 3

In this lesson, you will
- describe future events.
- interpret charts.

Planning for Retirement

🎧 **Listen and read the article about recent changes in Japan's working conditions.**

NEWSWIRE

JUNE 2001

Tomoki Sato can't wait until he can pack up the things in his office and never return to it. That day is coming up soon for him. Mr. Sato is one of the millions of aging Japanese workers who are approaching their retirement.

Japan's public and private pension systems face serious problems because of the nation's rapidly aging population. The Institute of Population Problems at the Ministry of Health and Welfare estimates that the number of people age 65 and older will nearly double by 2020, reaching 32 million. Senior citizens will make up about 25 percent of Japan's population, the highest proportion in any major industrial country.

Because return on investments has been low and the number of retirees has been rising, companies have been forced to increase employee pension-plan contributions.

There are two basic corporate pension schemes: employee pension funds, which are managed by outside organizations, and tax qualified pensions, managed by companies in-house. These pensions are completely separated from the public pension insurance system.

At retirement, employees are usually paid their pensions in one of three ways: lump sum, annuity (a portion each year), or a combination of the two. The current eligible age for public pension payments is 60.

Mr. Sato has already made plans for his days away from the corporate world. But he could not afford some of those plans if he were merely relying on his pension. Thanks to his wise investment strategies, he will have enough money to take a cruise or buy a farm.

▶**Pair** **What do you know about pension plans in your country? Discuss them with your partners and compare them with the system in Japan.**

1 After Tomoki retires, he's going to receive a pension.

Read the article on page 22 again. Then choose the best meaning for each of the words below.

1. retirement
   a. changing jobs
   b. stopping working

2. pension
   a. money a retiree is paid
   b. money a retiree is earning

3. senior citizen
   a. an old person
   b. a retired person

4. strategies
   a. military actions
   b. plans for success

5. cruise
   a. a plane trip
   b. a boat trip

2 Tomoki will take a cruise as soon as he retires.

Look at the pictures showing Tomoki's plans for his retirement and write sentences using *after*, *as soon as*, **or** *until*.

| **After** Tomoki **retires**, he's **going to buy** a farm. | Tomoki **can't take** a cruise **until** he **retires**. |

1. _____

2. _____

3. _____

4. _____

5. _____

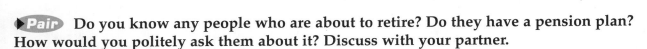

6. _____

▶ **Pair** Do you know any people who are about to retire? Do they have a pension plan? How would you politely ask them about it? Discuss with your partner.

3 I'm going to take it easy after I retire.

▶ **Pair** Complete the chart about yourself. Then ask your partner about his or her plans and write the responses in the chart. Share your responses with the class.

Example: What are you going to do **as soon as you get home today**?
I'm going to finish painting my room **as soon as I get home**.

Future plans	You	Your partner
as soon as you get home today		
until you go to bed tonight		
when you receive your degree		
until you find a job (or a better job)		
when you get married		
before you have children		
as soon as you retire		
(Your own phrase)		

4 Online

Log onto http://www.prenhall.com/brown_activities
The Web: Writing a Résumé
Grammar: What's your grammar IQ?
E-mail: What I've Done

5 Wrap Up

▶ **Pair** Look at the two charts below and answer the questions on page 25.

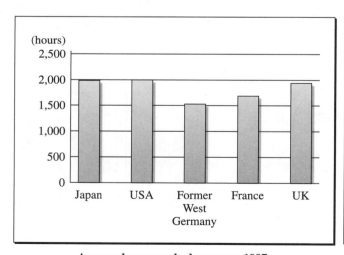

Average hours worked per year, 1997

Source:
http://jin.jcic.or.jp/stat/stats/09LAB42.html

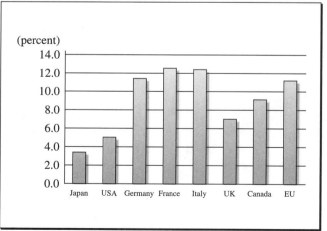

Unemployment rate, 1998

Source:
http://210.235.30.41/stat/stats/09LAB34.html

1. Which countries have the highest unemployment rate?

2. What's the unemployment rate in the United Kingdom?

3. Which two countries have the highest number of average working hours?

4. Which country has the lowest number of average working hours?

5. Search the Internet to find data about average annual working hours and the unemployment rate in your countries and make a chart for each one. Write statements comparing the data for the two countries. (If you are both from the same country, use the charts on this page for comparison.)

Strategies for Success

➤ **Practicing talking about routine activities**
➤ **Role-playing an interview situation**
➤ **Scanning for specific details**

1. With a partner, practice talking about your routine activities during the course of a year. Ask each other about the frequency of: eating out, getting exercise, inviting friends to your house, visiting parents/grand-parents, brothers/sisters, etc. Use the frequency adverbs in Lesson 2, Exercise 3.

2. With your partner, look for a newspaper (in English) that advertises different jobs. Pick two jobs you would like to apply for. Then, your partner role plays the employer by asking you questions about your experience. You ask your partner for more details about the job. Then switch roles.

3. The opener of Lesson 3 is an article about changes in Japan's working conditions. Practice your scanning skills by looking for:

    (a) the population of people 65 and older in 2020
    (b) two types of pension plans
    (c) three payment methods at retirement
    (d) what Mr. Sato will be able to do with his investments

CHECKPOINT

How much have you learned in this unit? Review the goals for each lesson. What skills can you confidently use now? What skills do you need to practice? List these below.

Skills I've Learned Well

_____

_____

_____

_____

Skills I Need to Practice

_____

_____

_____

_____

Learning Preferences

In this unit, which type of activity did you like the best and the least? Write the number in the box: 1 = best; 2 = next best; 3 = next; 4 = least.

- ❑ Working by myself
- ❑ Working with a partner
- ❑ Working with a group
- ❑ Working as a whole class

In this unit, which exercises helped you to learn to:

listen more effectively? Exercise _____   read more easily? Exercise _____

speak more fluently? Exercise _____   write more clearly? Exercise _____

Which exercise did you like the most? _____   Why? _____

Which exercise did you like the least? _____   Why? _____

Vocabulary

Nouns	Frequency Adverbs	Adverbs of Manner
cruise	always	beautifully
film processing	usually	carefully
freelance photographer	sometimes	cautiously
pension	never	easily
retiree		financially
retirement	**Verbs**	happily
strategies	handle	immensely
training	retire	quickly

GRAMMAR SUMMARY

Simple present vs. present continuous

> The process usually **goes** very quickly, but today it **is going** very slowly.

Present perfect

> How long **have** you **been** a film processor?
> I**'ve been** a film processor **for a year/since 1999**.

Placement of adverbs and prepositional phrases

Subject	Frequency	Verb	Direct Object	Manner	Place	Time
I		'm enjoying	it	immensely.		
He	always	reads	his letters		at home	in the morning.

Adverbial clauses with future time

> **After** Tomoki **retires**, he's **going to buy** a farm.
> Tomoki **can't take** a cruise **until** he **retires**.

COMMUNICATION SUMMARY

Requesting information

How long have you been a film processor?

Giving job-related information

I've been a film processor for two years.

Describing future events

After Tomoki retires, he's going to buy a farm.
Tomoki can't take a cruise until he retires.

Talking about habits

Yumiko usually wears a lab coat.

Talking about everyday activities

Yumiko works in the lab.

Describing the manner in which an action occurs

Oscar cooks meals expertly in a restaurant.

UNIT 3

Lesson 1

In this lesson, you will

- ask for and give information.
- talk about past experiences.
- determine the sequence of past events.
- state a purpose or reason.

I'm suffering from test anxiety.

🔊 **Listen and read.**

Tony: Do you know what I hate?

Sofia: No, Tony. What do you hate?

Tony: Tests. I don't see how I can go to the university.

Sofia: You'll have to pass the Test of English as a Foreign Language, the TOEFL. Then you might have to take other examinations. And that's before classes begin.

Tony: Yeah, I know what the TOEFL is, but I don't know how I can possibly pass it.

Sofia: What you have is a bad case of test anxiety. Think about the cover letter you have to write with your admission application and you won't feel so bad about the TOEFL.

Tony: But . . . I can be creative with a cover letter. Besides, I'll have you to help me write it. I have to take the TOEFL all by myself.

Sofia: Well, what's wrong with that? You need to know that stuff if you want to get into the university. Journalists are writers, you know.

Tony: Yeah, but I want to go into broadcast journalism.

Sofia: You've still got to know how sentences are put together. Anyway, the TOEFL is not going to be that difficult.

Tony: It won't be for you. You probably don't even need to study.

Sofia: Yes, I do, and if we don't get started, neither of us will pass. I wonder why we came here. We could have had this conversation in a coffee shop.

Tony: OK, I promise. I won't talk until I know every grammar rule.

Sofia: It's a deal.

▶**Group** Do you ever have test anxiety? What do you think causes it? Discuss how to deal with it.

1 Do you know where the TOEFL test is being given?

Tony is having a bad dream the night before the TOEFL test. Respond to his questions.

Where are they giving the TOEFL?

I don't know where they're giving it.

Where are they giving the TOEFL?	I don't know **where they're giving it.**
What time does it start?	
How can I find out?	
Who might be able to help me?	
Why is this happening to me?	

▶**Group** Have you ever had a bad dream the night before an important test? Tell the group what happened in your dream.

2 Do you know what my score is?

🔊 Tony and Sofia have **go**tten the results of their TOEFL. Listen to their conversation and write their scores in each section.

	Listening	Structure/Writing	Reading
Tony			
Sofia			

▶**Pair** Which is more valuable for a college student—writing skills or test-taking skills?

3 She aced the test.

Discuss the meaning of the words in context below. Then match the words on the left with the definitions on the right.

Do well	Not do well
Sofia **aced** the test.	Ida studied hard, but she **flunked** the test.
She passed **with flying colors**.	She **bombed** the test.
She **crammed** all night for the final and did well enough to **make the honor roll**.	She was a poor student. She **skipped** class and **blew off** all the tests.

<u> b </u> 1. to **ace** a test

_____ 2. to **bomb** a test

_____ 3. to pass **with flying colors**

_____ 4. to **skip** a class or meeting

_____ 5. to **cram** for a test something

_____ 6. to **flunk** a test or a class

_____ 7. to **make the honor roll**

_____ 8. to **blow off** a test

a. get a failing grade and not pass

b. get the best grade possible

c. have one's name on a list of superior students

d. get almost nothing correct on a test

e. fail to do something or not show up for

f. study very hard immediately before a test

g. fail to attend

h. do very well

Pair Use the expressions above to talk about your own experiences taking tests.

4 I passed with flying colors.

Read Tony's e-mail to Oscar. Then put the events in chronological order on page 31.

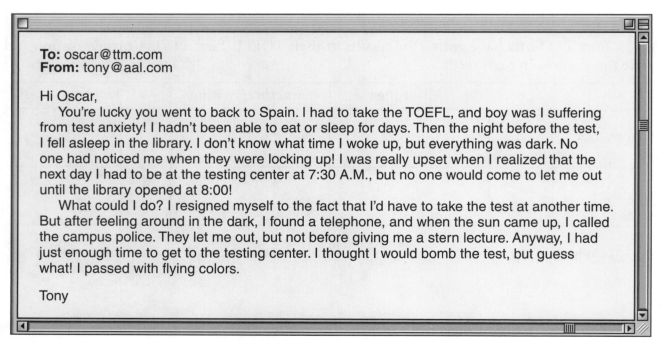

To: oscar@ttm.com
From: tony@aal.com

Hi Oscar,
    You're lucky you went to back to Spain. I had to take the TOEFL, and boy was I suffering from test anxiety! I hadn't been able to eat or sleep for days. Then the night before the test, I fell asleep in the library. I don't know what time I woke up, but everything was dark. No one had noticed me when they were locking up! I was really upset when I realized that the next day I had to be at the testing center at 7:30 A.M., but no one would come to let me out until the library opened at 8:00!
    What could I do? I resigned myself to the fact that I'd have to take the test at another time. But after feeling around in the dark, I found a telephone, and when the sun came up, I called the campus police. They let me out, but not before giving me a stern lecture. Anyway, I had just enough time to get to the testing center. I thought I would bomb the test, but guess what! I passed with flying colors.

Tony

First,   <u>Tony had trouble eating and sleeping.</u>

Next,   _____

After that,   _____

Then,   _____

Later,   _____

Finally,   _____

Afterward,   _____

▶ **Pair** Have you ever had a run of bad luck? Describe what happened.

5 I've always wanted to study medicine.

Read Sofia's application letter to the university and answer the questions.

Letter of Application

Dear Application Committee:

When I was a teenager, I had a dream that I was in the middle of a battlefield. There were wounded soldiers everywhere, and I was trying to help them. As I grew older, that dream kept coming back to me, and eventually I decided that my vocation was in medicine. I decided that the best thing I could do with my life would be to become a physician. If I am able to finish my education and become an M.D., I may not practice in a war zone, but I will certainly engage in battles for people's health.

A desire to help people is only one motivating factor for me, however. I also feel that I will be an effective doctor because I'm very much attracted to the science of medicine. I loved being behind the microscope in my high school science class, and I even like the smell of bleach in the hospital where I am a volunteer. I know that modern medicine is waging war against cancer and Parkinson's Disease, and I sincerely want to participate.

In order to prepare for a career in medicine, I have worked hard in school, been on the honor role every semester, and taken many science-based courses. I hope you will consider me a qualified applicant to your college.

Sincerely,

Sofia Mansoor

Sofia Mansoor

1.   What reasons does Sofia give for wanting to be a doctor? Do you think they are good reasons?

2.   Do you think Sofia will be a good doctor? Please explain your reasoning.

3.   What kind of medicine do you think she will practice? Why?

4.   Would this letter be appropriate in your culture? Why or why not?

▶ **Group** Do you think a story like the one about Sofia's dream is appropriate for an application letter to a college or university? Why or why not?

In this lesson, you will
- determine the sequence of past events.
- talk about past experiences.

I need some time to adjust.

🎧 **Listen and read.**

Steve: So how do you like the class?

Nelson: You mean the graphic design class? Oh, I love the class, but I need some time to adjust.

Steve: What do you mean?

Nelson: Well, I've never been in a class with Americans before.

Steve: Oh . . . I think I understand. It's a different culture. I'd probably feel the same if I were going to school in your country.

Nelson: Yes. Part of it is cultural, and part of it has to do with my English. When I'm with native speakers, I'm worried that I might make a mistake and be laughed at.

Steve: I think your English is very good. Of course you have an accent, but hey, who doesn't? How long had you studied English before you came here?

Nelson: For three years in high school, but I didn't learn much. It was kind of like the Spanish you learn here in high school.

Steve: I know what you mean. I had studied Spanish for a couple of years before I went to Mexico, but I had such a hard time communicating with people there. The nice thing about this class, though, is that most of it is hands-on, so you don't really have to talk much. By looking at your first assignment, I can tell you're very good at working on the computer.

Nelson: So are you.

Steve: I'm OK now, but I didn't know a thing about computers two years ago. Before I started my new job, I hadn't even touched a computer. I never thought I'd be interested in it.

Nelson: I hadn't had any experience with computers before I came here either. As soon as I arrived, though, I bought a used computer and started using it in my spare time. Now my love affair with the computer is really paying off.

▶ **Pair** What has your experience been in dealing with another culture or language? Can you relate to Nelson's feelings? What advice would you give to someone in Nelson's situation?

1 I hadn't even touched a computer.

Who do you think would say the following statements? Write *N* for Nelson and *S* for Steve.

1. I hadn't had a computer at home before I bought one here. [ ]

2. I've never been in a class with Americans before. [ ]

3. I'd never had a friend from another country before I met you. [ ]

4. I'd worked a little with a computer before taking this class. [ ]

5. I'd never thought I'd be good with computers before I started this class. [ ]

2 Nelson's English was good because he had studied at the World Language Center.

Read the following statements about Nelson. Write *1* for the event that happened first and *2* for the event that happened second. Then, combine the two statements, using *because*, *so (that)*, or *in order to*.

1. a. Nelson's English was good. [2]
   b. He studied English at the World Language Center. [1]

   Nelson's English was good **because** he had studied English at the World Language Center.

2. a. Nelson studied English. [1]
   b. He got a good job in the United States. [2]

   Nelson had studied English **in order to** get a good job in the United States.

3. a. Nelson studied design in his country. [ ]
   b. He found the concepts in the graphic design class easy. [ ]

   _____

4. a. Nelson learned about computers in his spare time. [ ]
   b. He got a job at a company as a website developer. [ ]

   _____

5. a. Nelson enjoyed working at the new company. [ ]
   b. He always wanted to work on websites. [ ]

   _____

6. a. Nelson made friends with one of his colleagues named Joe. [ ]
   b. He felt happier at his job. [ ]

   _____

3 Nelson had designed a simple website, but his client wanted a flashy one.

Yesterday, Nelson had just finished working on a website when his client, Mr. Franklin, called and requested a set of features that were different from what his partner had asked for. Read their conversation and combine both parts into one sentence.

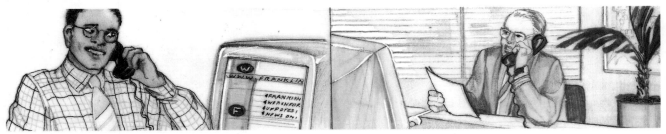

Nelson: I designed a simple title for the home page.

Mr. Franklin: I want a flashy title for the home page.

1. _Mr. Franklin wanted a flashy title for the home page, but Nelson had designed a simple one._

Nelson: I didn't put any animation in your website.

Mr. Franklin: Actually, I want some animation.

2. _____

_____

Nelson: I also didn't create links to any government agencies.

Mr. Franklin: I want a link to the Department of Transportation.

3. _____

_____

Nelson: I used navy blue and gray for your website.

Mr. Franklin: I want bright colors to attract customers.

4. _____

_____

Nelson: I put your picture on your website.

Mr. Franklin: I don't want my picture there.

5. _____

_____

Nelson: I didn't include any audio.

Mr. Franklin: I definitely want audio with loud sound effects.

6. _____

_____

4 A Brief History of the Internet

Read about the history of the Internet. Make a timeline of the events and then complete the sentences.

FRIDAY, SEPTEMBER 17, 1999

Computer News

In 1962, MIT's J. C. R. Licklider came up with the idea of a global computer network to share and access data and programs. Licklider became the head of the computer research program at the United States Department of Defense's Advanced Research Projects Agency (ARPA), which started and funded the Internet's development.

In 1967, Lawrence Roberts published his "Plan for the ARPAnet" computer network, proposing a design for a worldwide network.

By 1968, the development of the first hardware was well underway. In late 1969, the first tests were made at the University of California, Los Angeles (UCLA) and then at Stanford University. Over the next few years, the Internet continued to grow as government agencies, universities, and corporations continued to work on its development.

E-mail and the Internet were first presented in 1972 at the Internet Computer Communication Conference. The World Wide Web began in 1989.

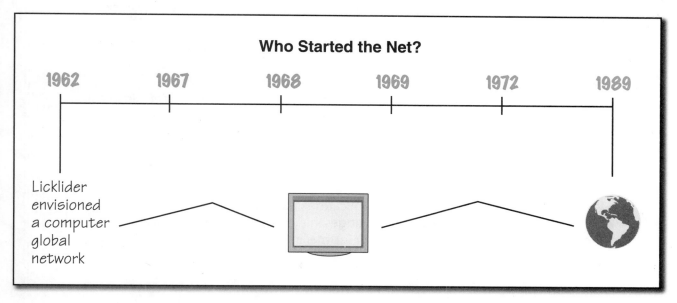

Who Started the Net?

| 1962 | 1967 | 1968 | 1969 | 1972 | 1989 |

Licklider envisioned a computer global network

1. By 1963, ___Licklider had already envisioned a global computer network.___

2. By 1968, _____.

3. In 1969, _____.

4. In 1972, _____.

5. In 1989, _____.

In this lesson, you will

- talk about getting/having something done.
- talk about making decisions.

CollegeLink.com

Read about how the Internet can help you apply to colleges.

College application deadlines are quickly approaching!

ARE YOU READY to fill out applications for your favored school, your second choice, your safety school, and a couple more "just to be sure?"

You've just found a better (and easier) way—have CollegeLink do it for you!

"Getting CollegeLink to submit my application once was a lot easier than filling out seven applications, and I got the school of my choice to accept me."

D.M., Student, Washington, DC

"Applying to college by computer makes sense for today's students and admission offices. That's why we—and so many other leading colleges and universities—welcome students who have the CollegeLink program prepare and submit their applications."

Michael Steidel, Director of Admission, Carnegie Mellon U.

Here's how we make the process FASTER and EASIER:

- We have you fill out our form once and select your schools.
- We transfer all your data onto the actual application forms of your schools.
- We e-mail or send your completed applications back to you for your review.
- We get you to make any necessary changes via your personal online account.
- We send your applications back to you for mailing to the colleges of your choice.
- **Real Video—Why you should apply online.**
  http://www.video.wsii.com/collegelink/whyapply3.ram

With CollegeLink, there is no service fee. With over 1,000 participating CollegeLink schools, you're sure to find the college you want. And CollegeLink.com is the only online application partnered with the College board, so you know you can trust it 100%!

Begin the Application Process at *http://www/collegelink.com/* Now!

Source: http://www.collegelink.com/

▶ **Pair** Do you think it's a good idea to apply to colleges online? Why or why not? Make a list of the advantages and disadvantages. Present your list to the class.

1 Have CollegeLink do it for you!

There are many ways to get something done for you. Look at these sentences from the reading.

> Ask: **Have** CollegeLink **do** it for you!
> Persuade: I **got** the school of my choice **to accept** me.
> Require: We **make** participating colleges **support** the cost of the service.

Pair There are three more examples in the reading. Find them and write them.

1. _____

2. _____

3. _____

2 Mrs. Silva made Tony finish his homework before he could watch TV.

Pair Look at the pictures and discuss what's happening.

1. When Tony was in elementary school, Mrs. Silva had a lot of rules for him. What did she make Tony do?

Finish your homework before watching TV.

Take the dog for a walk after dinner.

Brush your teeth before you go to bed.

2. When Tony was at the World Language Center, he was very busy, so he persuaded his classmate Ivan to help him. What did he get Ivan to do?

Ivan, could you do my laundry, please? You're going to the laundromat anyway.

Would you pick up my suit? You're going to the cleaners anyway.

Ivan, could you cash this check for me? You're going to the bank anyway.

3. Now, Tony lives alone. He doesn't have time to do some things, and he doesn't know how to do other things. What does he have other people do for him?

Please wash and wax my car.

Please paint the walls white.

Please deliver the paper every Sunday.

3 I'd get him to go and see the professor immediately.

▶ **Group** Decide what you would do in these situations. Then report your decisions to the group.

Example:

Your roommate wakes up late for a class on a test date. You persuade him to

    a. go and see the professor immediately, and tell him the truth.

    b. call the professor with an imaginative explanation for his absence.

    c. go back to sleep.

I'd get him to go and see the professor immediately and tell him the complete truth.

1.   Your roommate wants to join student organizations on campus, but she's afraid they will interfere with her studies. You advise her to

    a. sign up for the organizations she is interested in.

    b. sign up for those organizations that she's interested in plus 3 or 4 others.

    c. wait and sign up next year when she is better settled into college life.

2.   Your roommate's freshman-year grades are poor. You pursuade him to

    a. promise to improve them starting right now.

    b. make excellent grades his top priority for sophomore year, even if it means giving up social activities.

    c. give up on grades altogether and focus his attention on his soccer team.

3.   Your roommate is having problems with a group member who is not doing his fair share of the work on a class project. You persuade her to

    a. confront the group member.

    b. go on a hunger strike to protest the classmate's laziness.

    c. ask the professor to move her to a new group.

4.   Your roommate is sitting at her desk with a ton of homework piled in front of her. You convince her to

    a. clean her room before starting because it will help her to focus.

    b. dive into the work and stay focused.

    c. calm down and do the work one subject at a time.

5.   Spring break is right around the corner, and your roommate doesn't have any money. You advise him to

    a. find a job and work through the break.

    b. use his credit card to fly to Acapulco.

    c. use his creativity and plan a cheap road-trip with friends.

Based on: http://www.makingcollegecount.com/pwc/results.html

4 Online

Log onto http://www.prenhall.com/brown_activities
The Web: Taking a Test
Grammar: What's your grammar IQ?
E-mail: Ready or Not?

5 Wrap Up

Group Read and discuss the questions that follow.

In many countries, high school and university entrance exams are, by far, the most important determining factors of one's future role in society. The schools students get into and the scores they get on the exams are more important to prospective employers than their actual performance in college.

With such emphasis put on entrance exams, there is great pressure to perform well. Many students start studying for the high school entrance exams when they are in fourth grade. They say, "All you think about is study, study, study, so you can go to good schools and work for a good company." Success or failure on these exams practically determines their future.

1. Discuss the use of a single test as a way of selecting students. What are some other criteria that might be used for selecting students?

2. Do you think that excessive pressure to perform well on a test could lead to cheating? If someone were caught cheating in school in your country, what would the teacher do? What do you think the teacher should do?

Strategies for Success

➤ **Preparing for an English test**
➤ **Using strategies while taking a test**
➤ **Writing as a thinking process**

1. With a partner, or a group of 4–6 people, prepare for an English test that you'll be taking soon. Brainstorm some strategies for preparing for the test. Decide how you would do things like: (1) getting information about the test; (2) doing a systematic review; (3) forming a study group; and (4) doing practice exercises.

2. In the same group, make a list of successful strategies to use during the test. Include suggestions for: (1) reading directions carefully; (2) budgeting your time; and (3) avoiding careless errors.

3. In your journal, list several important decisions you will have to make in your life soon (changing jobs, applying for school, buying an expensive item, moving to a new place, etc.). Then, write a paragraph about each decision, in which you discuss the positive and negative aspects of each. If, after writing, you are now ready to make the final decision, write that and explain what convinced you.

CHECKPOINT

How much have you learned in this unit? Review the goals for each lesson. What skills can you confidently use now? What skills do you need to practice? List these below.

Skills I've Learned Well

_____

_____

_____

_____

Skills I Need to Practice

_____

_____

_____

_____

Learning Preferences

In this unit, which type of activity did you like the best and the least? Write the number in the box: 1 = best; 2 = next best; 3 = next; 4 = least.

❏ Working by myself   ❏ Working with a group

❏ Working with a partner   ❏ Working as a whole class

In this unit, which exercises helped you to learn to:

listen more effectively?   Exercise _____   read more easily?   Exercise _____

speak more fluently?   Exercise _____   write more clearly?   Exercise _____

Which exercise did you like the most? _____   Why? _____

Which exercise did you like the least? _____   Why? _____

Vocabulary

Verbs
adjust
cheat
intend
support

Nouns
application
behavior
entrance exam
link
TOEFL

Adjectives
flashy
hands-on

Transition Words
afterward
finally
first
later
next
then

Expressions
to ace a test
to blow off a test
to bomb a test
to cram for a test
to flunk a test
to make the honor roll
to pass with flying colors
to skip class

GRAMMAR SUMMARY

Embedded questions

I don't know I can't tell you	**where** **what time**	the **test is being given**. the **test starts**.

Past perfect

Nelson's English was good	because	he **had studied** English at the World Language Center.
I **hadn't had** any experience with computers	before	I **came** here.

Active causative

We We	**have** **make**	you colleges	**fill out** our form once. **support** the cost of the service.
I	**got**	the school of my choice	**to accept** me.

COMMUNICATION SUMMARY

Asking for and giving information

Do you know where the TOEFL test is being given?

No, I don't know where they're giving it.

Talking about past experiences

First, Tony had trouble eating and sleeping. Then, he fell asleep in the library.

I have never been in a class with Americans before.

Stating a purpose or reason

I also feel that I will be an effective doctor because I'm very much attracted to the science of medicine.

In order to prepare for a career in medicine, I have worked hard in school, been on the honor roll every semester, and taken many science-based courses.

Determining the sequence of past events

Before I started my new job, I hadn't even touched a computer.

Talking about getting/having something done

He gets Ivan to do his laundry.

He has the painter paint his living room.

Talking about making decisions

I'd get her to go to see the professor immediately and tell him the truth.

UNIT 4

Lesson 1

In this lesson, you will
- describe experiences.
- describe abilities and skills.

Starting Work

🔊 **Ivan has just completed a training program for help-desk technicians, and he's starting his new job at Sanchez Sports Design. He's getting some advice from Gina.**

Ivan: Hello.

Gina: Hi, Ivan. I'm sorry I cut you off, but I had to answer the other line.

Ivan: Oh, hi, Gina. Thanks for calling me back.

Gina: So you want some advice about your new job at Sanchez Sports Design?

Ivan: Yes, I was wondering how I can start off on the right foot, so to speak . . .

Gina: Well, from my own experience, companies want to find out if new employees can do the job and if they can get along with their coworkers and supervisors. Both are important.

Ivan: I guess the company thinks I can do the job since they hired me.

Gina: Yes, but to get ahead, you have to do your work well *and* on time. Companies also value people who are easy to get along with and responsible. The way you do your work and how you act can either make or break you.

Ivan: Well, what can I do to get ahead?

Gina: Your supervisor will usually show you how to do something. Listen carefully, watch, and then follow directions. If you don't understand, ask questions. If you're having trouble doing something, don't give up. And don't be afraid to ask others for help.

Ivan: I don't want to make mistakes, so I'd better face up to the fact that I need to be careful.

Gina: Right. Don't try to do too much too soon. And don't look down on your coworkers or supervisor. Above all, don't get into gossiping about the company, your supervisors, and coworkers.

Ivan: Gee, thanks, Gina. I knew I could count on you for sound advice.

▶ **Pair** **Why would a company want to know if you can work well with other people? Make one list of what you should do to start off well when you get a new job and another list of what you shouldn't do. Share your lists with the class.**

1 Thanks for calling me back.

▶**Pair** Refer to the conversation on page 42 and match the phrasal verbs with the definitions.

_____	1. cut off		a.	make progress
_____	2. call back		b.	fail to finish
_____	3. find out		c.	rely on
_____	4. get along with		d.	interrupt
_____	5. get ahead		e.	feel superior to
_____	6. give up		f.	participate in
_____	7. face up to		g.	discover
_____	8. look down on		h.	acknowledge something unpleasant or difficult
_____	9. get into		i.	return a telephone call
_____	10. count on		j.	have a friendly relationship with

2 Ivan called up his supervisor.

▶**Pair** Complete the paragraphs with the phrasal verbs from the box that have the same meaning as the words in parentheses. Use correct forms and tenses.

find out	look over	try out	write down	turn on
talk over	hang up	look up	call up	come over

After Ivan (1. *replaced the telephone receiver on its hook*), he (2. *telephoned*) his supervisor to see if they could (3. *discuss*) some of the duties of a help-desk technician. Ivan's supervisor told him to (4. *come to her office*) so she could (5. *discover*) how much Ivan already knew about the job.

First, Ivan's supervisor asked him to (6. *start*) the computer. She told Ivan he could (7. *examine*) the instructions in the user's manual. Then, she got Ivan to (8. *test*) the backup system. Finally, she informed him that he would be responsible for (9. *recording*) requests for phone support and (10. *seeking in a reference book*) technical information for the Network Management Team.

3 First, turn on the power.

Ivan's supervisor is giving him directions. Look at the different ways she gives them.

Turn on the power.
Turn the power **on.**
Turn it **on.**

Write down the requests.
Write the requests **down.**
Write them **down.**

Call up the supervisor.
Call the supervisor **up.**
Call her **up.**

Look up the products.
Look the products **up.**
Look them **up.**

▶**Pair** **Make sentences using the words in parentheses. How many different sentences can you make?**

1. Ivan *(call up/his supervisor)* to discuss his job.

2. Ivan's supervisor asked him to *(turn on/the computer).*

3. Then, she got Ivan to *(try out/the backup system).*

4. Ivan will be responsible for *(write down/requests)* for phone support.

5. Ivan has to *(look up/technical information)* for the Network Management Team.

6. Gina *(call back/Ivan).*

4 I warm up with a few leg and arm exercises.

Ivan is talking to Mario, a coworker, about what he does in his free time. Complete their conversation with one of the phrasal verbs from the list. Notice that none of the verbs are followed by an object.

Mario: You're looking healthy, Ivan. Do you run every day?

Ivan: Yes, and I also _____ at the gym several times a week.
₁

Mario: What do you do at the gym?

Ivan: I _____ with a few leg and arm exercises. Then I swim
₂
a few laps in the pool.

Mario: I guess you feel ready for work, then, don't you?

Ivan: Yes, but sometimes it wears me out. Then I have to

_____ and take a shower, and _____ for a while.
₃ ₄

Mario: I know what you mean. Have you ever _____ from too much exercise?
₅

Ivan: No, but once when I was a kid, I fainted from _____ too fast. I _____ right
₆ ₇
away, though.

Mario: You look a little pale right now. Would you like to _____?
₈

Ivan: No. I'm fine. I could _____ like this all day.
₉

---

come to

come to, *intr.v.*—to get one's consciousness back
go back, *intr.v.*—to return
go on, *intr.v.*—to continue
lie down, *intr.v.*—to lie on a bed or sofa
pass out, *intr.v.*—to lose consciousness
stand up, *intr.v.*—to stop sitting or lying; to take a standing position
sit down, *intr.v.*—to stop standing; to take a sitting position
warm up, *intr.v.*—to get ready; to exercise for a short time
work out, *intr.v.*—to exercise

5 Have you looked up a word in the dictionary recently?

Class Find out *who* has done these things recently and *when*.

Example:

A: **Have you** looked up a word in the dictionary recently?

B: **Yes, I have.** OR **No, I haven't.**

A: **When did you** look it up?

B: This morning.

Find someone who . . .	Who	When
1. has tried out a new product recently.		
2. has cut down on candy and desserts recently.		
3. has made up a homework assignment recently.		
4. has gotten over an illness recently.		
5. has called up a friend or relative recently.		
6. has worked out recently.		

6 I don't give up easily.

Group Discuss Ivan's mind map of skills. Which skills do you think he learned in the help-desk technician training? Which abilities did he already have? Decide if the job is right for him.

Group Make a mind map of your own strong points and categorize them into lists of skills and abilities. Share it with the group. Discuss the types of work you would qualify for.

Lesson 2

In this lesson, you will
- confirm information.
- make requests.
- accept requests.
- refuse requests.

Meeting the Boss!

Ivan is meeting his new boss, Mr. Sanchez, for the first time. Listen and read.

Mr. Sanchez: Come in, Ivan. Have a seat.

Ivan: Thanks.

Mr. Sanchez: How do you like your job so far?

Ivan: I love it. This is the kind of company I've always wanted to work for.

Mr. Sanchez: I'm glad to hear that. Is all your paperwork completed?

Ivan: No, sir. I have an orientation with Human Resources tomorrow. I guess we'll get it done there.

Mr. Sanchez: This is your first job as a help-desk technician, isn't it?

Ivan: Yes, it is. I just finished my training about a month ago. I came here from Russia a couple of years ago.

Mr. Sanchez: Interesting. I have a brother who used to work in Kiev in Ukraine.

Ivan: Oh, I have relatives in Ukraine. How long did he work there?

Mr. Sanchez: For a couple of years. Would you mind if I gave him your e-mail address? I'm sure he'd like to talk with you.

Ivan: I wouldn't mind at all.

Mr. Sanchez: I come from Mexico myself, so I know how it feels to live and work in a new country. It takes a while to feel completely adjusted. I've been here about ten years now.

Ivan: Yes . . . but it's been a great learning experience for me.

Mr. Sanchez: I'm sure it has. Well, listen. Let me know if there's anything I can do to help. My door is always open.

Ivan: Thank you, sir.

Mr. Sanchez: You're welcome. It's been nice to meet you.

▶ **Pair** **What do you think about the interaction between Mr. Sanchez and Ivan? Is the conversation formal or informal? How would you feel if you were Ivan?**

1 Would you please fill out these forms?

Susan in Human Resources is asking Ivan for various items. Write a polite request for each item.

Polite requests

Would you mind filling out these two forms?	**Please** fill out these two forms.
Could you please fill out these two forms?	**Would you please** fill out these two forms?

1. (fill out) forms   <u>Would you please fill out these two forms</u> ?

2. green card   _____ ?

3. official transcripts   _____ ?

4. (sign) forms   _____ ?

5. a photo   _____ ?

6. a canceled check   _____ ?

2 Would you mind explaining the procedure for taking vacations?

Pair Ivan has gone back to Human Resources to give Susan his documents and ask her some questions. Look at the list of benefits that Ivan has questions about. Make polite requests using *would you, could you, would you mind, could you please,* and *would you please.*

Questions about	Polite requests
1. procedure for taking vacations	**Would you mind** explaining the procedure for taking vacations?
2. health insurance	**Could you please** tell me more about my health insurance?
3. sick leave	
4. paid holidays	
5. work hours	
6. overtime	
7. bonus	
8. retirement plan	
9. (other)	

3 Ivan's Benefits Package

🔊 Listen as Susan explains Ivan's benefits package. Under Ivan's name, write notes about each of the benefits listed.

	Ivan
1. vacation	2 weeks
2. health insurance	
3. sick leave	
4. paid holidays	
5. work hours	
6. overtime	
7. bonus	
8. retirement plan	
9. (other)	

▶Pair Using the expressions for polite requests from Exercises 1 and 2, interview two people who work at your school about their job benefits.

4 Ivan works in a sportswear design company, doesn't he?

▶Pair Read these statements about Ivan. Complete each statement with a tag question. Your partner will respond to the question based on what he or she knows about him.

1. Ivan works in a sportswear design company, _____?

2. Ivan wasn't born in the United States, _____?

3. Ivan is satisfied with the benefits in his new job, _____?

4. Ivan has health insurance with his new company, _____?

5. Ivan doesn't live with his family, _____?

5 Small Talk

Pair Make a polite request in the following situations. Then, your partner will respond to your request with the appropriate expression.

Accepting requests	Refusing requests
Yeah, no problem.	No, I'm sorry.
You bet.	I'm afraid I can't.
Sure.	I'd like to, but I can't.
I'd be glad to.	I would if I could, but I can't.
Of course.	I wish I could.
No, my pleasure.	
No, not at all.	

Example:

A: Could you close the window, please?

B: **Of course.** OR **No, I'm sorry.** It's too hot in here.

Lesson 3

In this lesson, you will

- talk about past events that are continuing into the present.
- talk about technology.

Why I Hate E-mail

 Listen and read.

The National Worker

June 21, 2000

Why I Hate E-mail
by Beverly Marks

*E*ver since e-mail came into my life, things have been getting progressively worse at the office. Sure e-mail makes it more convenient, but convenient for whom exactly? Certainly not me. My former identity as a one-thing-at-a-time goof-off is gradually being replaced by a multi-tasking fiend.

Ever since the beeping red light started announcing "you've got mail," I have been learning more about company policy and issues; I have been working longer hours; I've been staying later at the office; and darn it, I have become more efficient. This may be good for the company, but it sure does take a lot out of me.

E-mail means my superiors can send me memos in seconds, and they can prove that I received them. E-mail means I have to think up creative new ways of pretending that I have not gotten instructions or documents that I should have read before a certain meeting. "Sorry, my computer crashed" will only work so many times. And not only do my various bosses have better lines of communication with me, but I am also expected to respond to them in grammatical English. I miss the old days of the phone call when I could get through a conversation without having to worry about where I'm putting my commas.

E-mail has also severely diminished gossip time at the water cooler. I used to enjoy hearing about my colleagues' misadventures in boardroom meetings and out in the field, but now my colleagues keep large bottles of water on their desks, and all personal information comes electronically. However, due to the public nature of e-mail, I no longer get the juicy bits. Instead, I receive cautiously worded announcements. But, once in a while, I would like to laugh the way I did when Rita from Accounting told the story of the executive who showed up at an important presentation wearing two different-colored shoes.

Beverly Marks lives, works, and writes e-mail in St Louis, Missouri.

▶ **Group** Do you think the article is humorous? Discuss why you do or don't.

1 People have been shopping online.

Read the following statements and write *A* if you agree and *D* if you disagree. Then give some reasons to support your choice. Share your responses with the class.

Example: People have been shopping on the Internet more and more.
   (A)   _It is easier to compare prices. People don't leave home._

1. People have been spending more money on technology and related services in recent years.
   ( ) _____

2. Office workers have been accomplishing more in less time due to new technology.
   ( ) _____

3. The time that families spend together has been increasing because of new developments in technology.
   ( ) _____

2 She has been sending more e-mails.

▶**Pair**   Describe how Shelley's life has changed since she got e-mail.

Shelley **has been sending** e-mail more often than she used to.
She **has not been using** the phone as often as she used to.

▶**Class**   Has your life changed recently? Tell the class about something that you have been doing more often than you used to.

3 I design websites.

   Listen to Ivan and Nelson talking about their jobs. Then read the statements. Write *I* next to the tasks Ivan performs. Write *N* next to the ones that Nelson performs. Write *I/N* if they both do the task.

1. _____ I help different departments inside the company to solve their technology problems.

2. _____ I design websites.

3. _____ I maintain websites.

4. _____ I train people to use new technology.

5. _____ I have to do whatever the client wants.

▶**Group** Listen to the cassette again. What does Ivan like about his job? What does Nelson like?

4 Online

Log onto http://www.prenhall.com/brown_activities
The Web: Technical Terms
Grammar: What's your grammar IQ?
E-mail: What's Been Happening

5 Wrap Up

Discuss the responses to Ivan's questionnaire. Do you agree with his ideas for solving the problems?

How can the help desk help you?

I am in sales and I have to impress clients. But lately I've been having a hard time maintaining their interest. Is there some technology that can make me look good?

Workshop on presentation software?

How can the help desk help you?

Folks in our department have been having trouble communicating since we opened up a branch across town. People are not getting all their calls. Can you help?

Suggest an e-mail system.

▶ **Group** Here are two more responses. How would you solve these problems?

How can the help desk help you?

I don't know how to get on the Internet. I am very embarrassed about asking anyone because I feel I should know. Please help.

How can the help desk help you?

My computer is too slow. I have to wait a long time for it to do anything! Is there anything that can be done to make it faster?

Strategies for Success

➤ Using e-mail to practice proofreading skills
➤ Figuring out idioms and slang inductively
➤ Writing a narrative to practice a grammatical pattern

1. If you are doing the "Online" sections at the end of each chapter, the next time you write an e-mail message, carefully proofread it before you send it. Try to correct any grammar or spelling errors you have made, and make a note of those errors. Try to learn from those mistakes the next time you write.

2. With a partner, look at the article at the beginning of Lesson 3. It contains some idioms that might be difficult. List them, and using either context or a dictionary, find out what they mean. Then use them in a new sentence. Examples of idioms in the article: goof-off, multi-tasking fiend, darn it, take a lot out of me, crashed, lines of communication, gossip time at the water cooler, juicy bits.

3. For your journal, look at the list of phrasal verbs in Lesson 1, Exercise 1. Make up a story in which you use as many (possibly all) of the phrasal verbs as possible, and even more. For example, your story might start with this: "I *get along* well *with* David, but one day . . . "

CHECKPOINT

How much have you learned in this unit? Review the goals for each lesson. What skills can you confidently use now? What skills do you need to practice? List these below.

Skills I've Learned Well

_____

_____

_____

_____

Skills I Need to Practice

_____

_____

_____

_____

Learning Preferences

In this unit, which type of activity did you like the best and the least? Write the number in the box: 1 = best; 2 = next best; 3 = next; 4 = least.

❏ Working by myself   ❏ Working with a group

❏ Working with a partner   ❏ Working as a whole class

In this unit, which exercises helped you to learn to:

listen more effectively?   Exercise _____   read more easily?   Exercise _____

speak more fluently?   Exercise _____   write more clearly?   Exercise _____

Which exercise did you like the most? _____   Why? _____

Which exercise did you like the least? _____   Why? _____

Vocabulary

Nouns
client
Internet
software (program)

Verbs
acknowledge
faint
gossip
train

Separable Phrasal Verbs
call back   look up
call up   make up
cut off   talk over
figure out   try out
find out   turn on (off)
give up`   warm up
hang up   write down
look over

Polite Requests
Would you mind . . . ?
Would/Could you please . . . ?

Inseparable Phrasal Verbs
come over   go back
come to   go on
count on   lie down
cut down (on)   pass out
get ahead   sit down
get along   stand up
  (with)   work out
get over

Phrasal verbs

Separable	Inseparable
Turn on the power. **Turn** the power **on**. **Turn** it **on**.	I **work out** at the gym several times a week. I could **go on** like this all day. She's just **gotten over** a bad cold.

Present perfect continuous

Affirmative and negative statements

People	**have**	**been**	**shopping**	on the Internet	more and more.
She	**has not [hasn't]**		**using**	the phone	as much as she used to.

Information questions

How long	**have**	people	**been**	**shopping**	on the Internet?
Why	**has**	Ms. Marks		**sending**	e-mails?

Describing experiences
I work out at the gym several time a week.
I warm up with a few leg and arm exercises.

Describing abilities and skills
Ivan gets along with most people.
He's good at analyzing problems.

Making requests
Would you please fill out these two forms?
Would you mind explaining the procedure for taking vacations?

Confirming information
Ivan is satisfied with the benefits in his new job, isn't he?
Ivan doesn't live with his family, does he?

Accepting requests
I'd be glad to.
Of course.

Refusing requests
No, I'm sorry.
I'm afraid I can't.

Talking about past events that are continuing into the present
She has been sending e-mail more often than she used to.
She has not been using the phone as often as she used to.

UNIT 5

Lesson 1

In this lesson, you will
- describe a predicament.
- give opinions.
- identify people, places, and things.

A Learning Experience

Ivan is talking to Mr. Sanchez after his first technical assisting job. He had a hard time trying to fix the sales manager's computer.

Mr. Sanchez: Ivan, have you finished fixing Rick Dillon's computer yet?

Ivan: Is he the sales manager?

Mr. Sanchez: Yes, the one who reported that he couldn't open his files.

Ivan: Well, I had a really hard time trying to fix his computer.

Mr. Sanchez: Why's that?

Ivan: First of all, I tried the disk that was in the computer.

Mr. Sanchez: And?

Ivan: I got an error message. So I asked him if he had any other disks, and he pointed to a diskette box that was on the bookcase.

Mr. Sanchez: I see.

Ivan: But when I tried another disk, I still got an error message.

Mr. Sanchez: So what did you do?

Ivan: Well, I rebooted the computer and tried again, but I got the same error message. Then I tried a computer that was in the next office, but the same thing happened.

Mr. Sanchez: Ivan, do you remember the woman I introduced you to in my office last week? Judith Wu?

Ivan: Yes?

Mr. Sanchez: Well, she has a manual that I want you to look at. Look up the section that deals with magnetic media. Then come back and tell me what the problem was.

Ivan: I'm on my way, Mr. Sanchez.

Mr. Sanchez: By the way, Ivan, don't ever hesitate to talk to me about a problem. My door is always open.

Ivan: Thanks, Mr. Sanchez.

Mr. Sanchez: And Ivan, we appreciate the work you're doing for us. You're a valued member of our team.

Pair Have you ever found yourself in a predicament like Ivan's? Tell your partner about it.

1 Here's some more work.

▶Pair Look at the popular cartoon *Dilbert*. Who do you think has a better boss—Ivan or Dilbert? Why? In your opinion, what are the characteristics of a good boss? Make a list and read it to the class.

DILBERT reprinted by permission of United Feature Syndicate, Inc.

2 Rick Dillon is the sales manager who can't open his documents.

Identify the employees from the opening conversation and Exercise 1. Match the person in the left-hand column with the best description in the right-hand column. Then ask and answer questions to identify the people.

Example:

A: Who's the salesman who can't open his documents?

B: Rick Dillon is the sales manager who can't open his documents.

1. Rick Dillon is the sales manager ___c___
2. Mr. Sanchez is the boss _____
3. Ivan is the technician _____
4. Judith Wu is the woman _____
5. Dilbert is the cartoon character _____
6. Dilbert's boss is the person _____

a. who is helping Ivan out of a predicament.
b. who is giving Dilbert more work.
c. who can't open his documents.
d. that is having his blood pressure taken.
e. who is trying to fix Rick Dillon's computer.
f. who has a computer manual.

3 Ivan works for a company that designs sportswear.

▶Pair Combine the pair of sentences into one sentence. Then ask and answer questions using *What kind of.*

Example:

A: What kind of company does Ivan work for?

B: He works for a company that designs sportswear.

1. Ivan works for a company. The company designs sportswear.
2. Mr. Sanchez has a job. It's very interesting.
3. Rick sells tennis shoes. The tennis shoes are comfortable and inexpensive.
4. Judith writes reports. The reports are clear and concise.
5. Maria designs web pages. The web pages advertise the company's products.

4 The man who is the sales manager used to work in a department store.

Look at the list of employees who work at Sanchez Sports Designs. Ivan is telling Gina about them. Listen and write what they did before.

Employee	Present job	Previous job
1. Rick Dillon	sales manager	worked in a department store
2. Carlos Sanchez	owns the company	
3. Ben Yakamura	boss's assistant	
4. Susan Sullivan	supervises the Human Resources Department	
5. Sara Gleason	receptionist	
6. Maria Artiga	designs web pages	
7. Judith Wu	heads the Network Management Team	
8. Cindy Hoffart	office manager	

5 People who work in sales often have frustrating jobs.

Group Give your opinion about the different career areas and professions of the people in Exercise 4. Agree, partially agree, or disagree with your classmates' opinions.

Example:

A: People who work in sales often have frustrating jobs.

Agree B: Oh, I agree completely. OR
     I think you're right.

Disagree B: Oh, I disagree. I'm sure that salespeople have jobs that are very satisfying.

Agree in part B: I'm not sure that's true for everybody. OR
     You're probably right, but I'm sure some salespeople have jobs that are satisfying.

6 Judith is the person who(m) Mr. Sanchez introduced last week.

Pair Look at the notes Ivan has written about his coworkers and the tasks he has to do. Then use the information from the notes to make up sentences.

Examples:

> Judith is the computer specialist (who[m]) Mr. Sanchez introduced last week.
> Judith has the computer manual (that) Ivan needs to consult.

Notes

Judith, computer specialist
—Mr. Sanchez introduced her last week
—has computer manual I need to consult

Cindy, office manager
—had lunch with her yesterday
—has the tax forms I need to fill out

Ben, assistant
—Mr. Sanchez hired him right out of college
—has catalogs for computer parts I need to order

Rick, sales manager
—I tried to help yesterday
—has computer disks I couldn't open

7 I'd like someone who's creative.

What qualities would you like your partner for a school project to have? Look at the chart and rank them in the order of importance, from 1 = most important to 8 = least important, in the second column.

Qualities	My answers	Group answers
1. flexible		
2. creative		
3. talkative		
4. quiet		
5. dependable		
6. careful		
7. organized		
8. outgoing		

Group As a group, come to a consensus as to which quality is the most important and which is the least important. Give the group rankings in the third column of the chart and report your choices to the class.

In this lesson, you will
- give advice.
- suggest alternatives.
- compliment a person.

Trial and Error

🔊 **Ivan and Mr. Sanchez continue to discuss the problem with Rick Dillon's computer. Listen and read.**

Mr. Sanchez: Did you get the book from Ms. Wu, Ivan?

Ivan: No, I went to get it, but she wasn't in her office.

Mr. Sanchez: You could've left her a message.

Ivan: Yes, I guess I could have. But I did figure out the problem.

Mr. Sanchez: Great. So what was the problem?

Ivan: There was nothing wrong with the computer. The problem was with the diskette.

Mr. Sanchez: The diskette?

Ivan: Yes, you see, the diskette I was using was damaged, probably because it'd been sitting in bright sunshine.

Mr. Sanchez: I see.

Ivan: And when I tried another diskette, it was from the same box sitting in direct sunlight.

Mr. Sanchez: So how did you finally figure out the problem?

Ivan: I got one of my own diskettes that I was sure was fine and tried it on Mr. Dillon's computer, and it worked. I should've known better.

Mr. Sanchez: You did what I would've done. You followed a trial-and-error pattern.

Ivan: Thank you, Mr. Sanchez. Oh, I'm just curious . . . you knew what was wrong, didn't you?

Mr. Sanchez: Yes, I did, and I could've told you right there, but l wanted you to figure it out yourself. Frankly, I wanted to test your problem-solving skills.

Ivan: And did I pass?

Mr. Sanchez: You sure did, Ivan. You sure did.

▶ **Pair** When you are faced with solving a problem, do you try to resolve it by yourself or do you immediately ask for help? What steps do you take to resolve it? Discuss what to do with your partner.

1 He should have used the manual.

Read each statement and decide whether *he* refers to Ivan, Mr. Sanchez, or Mr. Dillon.

1. He could have resolved the problem for Ivan.   _Mr. Sanchez_
2. He must have left the diskettes in direct sunlight.   _____
3. He could have used the manual to resolve the problem.   _____
4. He could have left a message for Ms. Wu.   _____
5. He must have known right away that the diskettes were damaged. _____

2 Ivan shouldn't have done that!

Pair Ivan made several mistakes during the first couple of weeks at his new job. Now he is in a chat room on the Internet, telling others about those mistakes. Participate in the chat room and give him advice or make suggestions.

You *could have asked* your coworkers what they usually do before you bought the gift.	You *should have waited* at least a year before asking for a raise.
You *shouldn't have bought* an expensive gift for your boss because you're not close friends.	You *shouldn't have asked* for a raise right after starting your new job.

Ivan: I bought an expensive gift for my boss on his birthday, while my coworkers just signed a birthday card for him. I felt embarrased.	**YOU:**
Ivan: I called my boss at home to ask for a day off.	**YOU:**
Ivan: I sent a personal e-mail to everyone at work by mistake.	**YOU:**
Ivan: I yelled at Mr. Dillon for leaving the diskettes sitting in the sunlight.	**YOU:**
Ivan: I told a colleague to fix his computer problems himself because I was too busy. He reported that to Mr. Sanchez.	**YOU:**
Ivan: I printed my cousin's school assignment at work, and Mr. Sanchez found it in the printer.	**YOU:**

3 Ivan shouldn't have been in such a hurry.

Each of the pictures shows a situation that Ivan faced during his first week at his job. Write a statement about each one using *could have, should have, shouldn't have,* or *might have*.

Ivan **shouldn't have been** in such a hurry.	Ivan **could have set** the alarm.
Ivan **should have been** more careful.	Ivan **could have gotten** some help if he had asked his boss.

Ivan dropped the computer he was carrying.

1. _____

Ivan was late for work during the first week.

2. _____

Ivan went to an office party overdressed.

3. _____

Ivan argued with a colleague who needed help with her computer.

4. _____

Once Ivan fell asleep at work.

5. _____

Ivan used his company's copier to copy his personal documents.

6. _____

▶ **Pair** Have you done something in the past year that you regret now? Tell your partner about it and ask for suggestions or advice.

4 Regrets

▶**Pair** We all make mistakes. Look at the categories and talk about a mistake that you made in the past. Describe the situation and ask your partner for advice or suggestions.

Category	Specific situation	Advice or suggestion
1. Friends	I forgot my best friend's birthday because I was too busy.	You should have written it down on your calendar.
2. Family		
3. School		
4. Work		
5. Your own category		

5 Small Talk

▶**Pair** Give a compliment in each situation. More than one expression might be appropriate in some situations.

Phrases	Sentences
Good for you! Way to go! Congratulations! Good job!	I would've done the same. You did the right thing. You've outdone yourself. I couldn't have done it better.

1. I got a scholarship to the college I've always wanted to attend. _____

2. I fixed the car all by myself. _____

3. Look! I rearranged the furniture. What do you think? _____

4. I finished the paper before it was due. _____

5. I've never missed a class. _____

6. I apologized to my friend for not remembering his birthday. _____

7. I volunteered at the homeless shelter last weekend. _____

8. (Your own idea) _____

▶**Class** Tell the class about something positive that you did recently.

Lesson 3

In this lesson, you will
- draw conclusions.
- emphasize.
- make excuses.
- apologize.

E-mail Connections Unlimited

 Listen and read the following ad.

Find True Love in the Comfort of Your Own Home
Read three stories of e-mail romance and draw your own conclusions.

Jeanette Harrison is flying to England next week to take up permanent residence as Mrs. Robert Elliot. "One year ago, if you had told me that I was going to marry an Englishman and move to London, I would have laughed in your face," said the future Mrs. Elliot, who currently resides in Pocatello, Idaho. "But that's not true any longer. Thanks to E-mail Connections Unlimited, I'm going to start a whole new life." Ms. Harrison says she thoroughly enjoyed her online courtship of eight months. "We wrote to each other every day and sometimes more than once a day. "You can really get to know a lot about the person that way. By the time Robert flew out to Pocatello to meet me, I was pretty sure that he was the one."

Anthony Mari, of Carson City, Nevada, says that he had given up on regular dating services. "I used to use the newspaper ads, but not anymore. I would go out with a different girl every couple of weeks, but none of them worked out because I wasn't ready to get serious. So, not only did I feel bad about not calling the girl back, but I would also see her around town sometimes, which was usually embarrassing, if not totally awkward. As a result, I like the idea of getting to know someone anonymously. My e-mail connection may sit next to me on the bus and never know who I am unless we decide to take it to the next level.

"I hate blind dates, I hate singles bars, and I'm too busy to take a class or any of those other social activities that people suggest," says Lucille Kinkaid, a literature teacher from Baton Rouge, Louisiana, who is currently involved with a bookstore owner. "Basically, if I hadn't discovered E-mail Connections, I'd still be alone with my books. But I don't feel alone any longer. Not only does Adrian share my love of literature, but he also has a wonderful way with language. When we met in person for the first time, I actually suggested that we continue to e-mail because I enjoy reading his messages so much."

▶ **Pair** Have you ever met anyone through the Internet? Would you like to? What would be the advantages and/or disadvantages?

1 She might be shy.

Read the advertisement for E-mail Connections Unlimited on page 63 again. Write the name of the person who fits in the blank.

1. _____ might be shy.
2. _____ must be able to adjust to new situations.
3. _____ probably doesn't want to get married.
4. _____ is probably not interested in getting to know many new people.
5. _____ might live in a small town where many people know one another.
6. _____ must have a house full of books.
7. _____ must not like to date a variety of people.

▶Group **What conclusions can you draw about people who prefer to get to know each other through e-mail?**

2 Not only do I work 10 hours a day, but I also study at night.

Tony is using his work computer to write an e-mail message about himself for an online dating service. Look at the pictures and write additional sentences about Tony.

> **Not only** do I work 10 hours a day, **but I'm also** a student.
> **Not only** can I play guitar, **but I can also** paint.
> **Not only** am I intelligent, **but I am also** good-looking.

1. _____
_____
_____
_____

2. _____
_____
_____
_____

3. _____
_____
_____
_____

3 I won't use my computer for personal e-mail any longer.

Tony accidentally sent his e-mail message to a company distribution list. Now his boss and coworkers have read it. Read Tony's apologies and answer the questions.

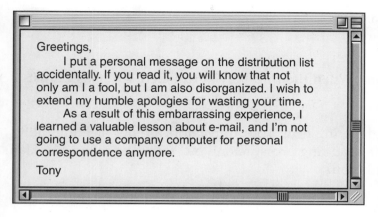

Greetings,

I put a personal message on the distribution list accidentally. If you read it, you will know that not only am I a fool, but I am also disorganized. I wish to extend my humble apologies for wasting your time.

As a result of this embarrassing experience, I learned a valuable lesson about e-mail, and I'm not going to use a company computer for personal correspondence anymore.

Tony

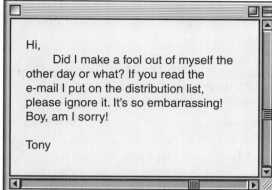

Hi,

Did I make a fool out of myself the other day or what? If you read the e-mail I put on the distribution list, please ignore it. It's so embarrassing! Boy, am I sorry!

Tony

- Which message goes to his boss?
- Which message goes to his coworkers?
- What differences do you notice between the two messages?
- Would these apologies be the same or different in your culture?

4 I'm sorry I'm late. I had to stop at the bank.

Look at the pictures and write an apology for each one.

1.   I apologize. I was delayed at work.

2. _____

3. _____

5 Online

Log onto http://www.prenhall.com/brown_activities
The Web: Meeting Someone
Grammar: What's your grammar IQ?
E-mail: It didn't have to happen.

6 Wrap Up

Group Role play the following situation. When the role-play is finished, Mr. Nash must decide how to solve the problem.

Mr. Nash: You are a supervisor for an engineering firm. Your translators are not meeting the deadlines, and the company president is putting pressure on you. You have asked Ms. Han, Mr. Reade, and Ms. Hulce to meet with you.

Ms. Han: You work as a translator for the company. You have not been feeling well, and you have to take a lot of breaks to rest.

Mr. Reade: You work as a translator for the company. You don't think you should have to do extra work just because Ms. Han is ill.

Ms. Hulce: You are Mr. Nash's assistant. Everyone comes to you with their problems because you are a good listener. As a result, people are always interrupting you and you can't get your work done.

Mr. Hanson: You are Mr. Nash's friend. He tells you his problem and you give him advice.

Strategies for Success

➤ **Complimenting others**
➤ **Listening, note-taking, and giving opinions**
➤ **Reviewing your goals**

1. With a partner, look at the list of compliments in Lesson 2, Exercise 5. Think of things you have accomplished and tell them to your partner. Your partner should respond, complimenting you using a different phrase or sentence each time.

2. Agree with a partner to watch the same TV show—something like a comedy or a soap opera. Take notes on what you liked and didn't like about it. Then, when you get together, exchange opinions about the show. Be sure to support your opinions with what you actually observed on the show.

3. Look back at the goals you set for yourself in Unit 1 (Strategies exercise 1). Have you reached some of them? Should you change some of them? Should you try harder? Write your thoughts in your journal.

CHECKPOINT

How much have you learned in this unit? Review the goals for each lesson. What skills can you confidently use now? What skills do you need to practice? List these below.

Skills I've Learned Well

_____

_____

_____

_____

Skills I Need to Practice

_____

_____

_____

_____

Learning Preferences

In this unit, which type of activity did you like the best and the least? Write the number in the box: 1 = best; 2 = next best; 3 = next; 4 = least.

❑ Working by myself

❑ Working with a partner

❑ Working with a group

❑ Working as a whole class

In this unit, which exercises helped you to learn to:

listen more effectively?   Exercise _____

speak more fluently?   Exercise _____

read more easily?   Exercise _____

write more clearly?   Exercise _____

Which exercise did you like the most? _____   Why? _____

Which exercise did you like the least? _____   Why? _____

Vocabulary

Nouns	Adjectives	Verbs	Complimentary Expressions
accounting	concise	apologize	Good for you!
compliment	creative	be delayed	Way to go!
office manager	dependable	design	Good job!
receptionist	flexible	volunteer	Congratulations!
sales manager	frustrating		
specialist	organized		
sportswear	outgoing		
technician	overdressed		
translator	quiet		
	talkative		

GRAMMAR SUMMARY

Relative clauses

Relative pronouns as subjects

Ivan is the **technician**	**who/that**	is trying to fix Rick's computer.

Ivan works for a **company**	**which/that**	designs sportswear.

Relative pronouns as objects

Judith is the **computer specialist**	**(who[m]/that)**	Mr. Sanchez introduced last week.

Judith has the computer manual	**(which/that)**	Ivan needs to consult.

Modals of advice or suggestions about the past

He	**could**	**have**	resolved	the problem for Ivan.
	should/shouldn't		left	a message for Ms. Wu.

Not only . . . but (also)

Not only do I work 10 hours a day, **but** I'm **also** a student.

COMMUNICATION SUMMARY

Describing a predicament
But when I tried another disk, I still got an error message.

Giving opinions
People who work in sales have frustrating jobs.

Identifying people, places, and things
Rick is a sales manager who used to work in a department store.
Cindy has the tax forms I need to fill out.

Giving advice
You should've written it down on your calendar.

Drawing conclusions
She might be shy.
She must have a house full of books.

Complimenting
Good for you!
I couldn't have done better.

Emphasizing
Not only do I work ten hours a day, but I'm also a student.

Apologizing
I'm sorry.
I wish to extend my humble apologies for wasting your time.

Making excuses
I'm sorry I'm late. I had to stop at the bank.

Lesson 1

In this lesson, you will
- talk about conditions.
- ask for advice.
- give advice.

Coping at Work

🔊 **Listen and read.**

Nelson: I'm glad Gina got these tickets. I wouldn't have had time to even think about going out if she hadn't called.

Lynn: Busy, huh?

Nelson: Yeah, I'm either working or sleeping.

Lynn: You don't sound happy.

Nelson: I'm going nuts! I've got to finish three websites by the end of next week! I need some support, but everyone they send to help me is incompetent. I don't know what to do.

Lynn: What do you mean, everyone is incompetent?

Nelson: I mean they don't know what they're doing. I have to teach them everything. What would you do in my situation?

Lynn: I don't know what I'd do in your situation. But when I have to work with new people, I always take the time to get to know them. If we can establish a good working relationship, I find it easier to make the projects go more smoothly.

Nelson: How do you find the time?

Lynn: Either I postpone something that's less important or I stay late. Once in a while I do both.

Nelson: Hmm, I'm used to figuring out everything by myself. Maybe I should come to you for advice more often.

▶ **Group** **When you have to work on a project, do you prefer to do things by yourself, or do you like to have the support of a team? Tell the group the reasons for your preference.**

1 If you work late too often, you should do some work on your schedule.

▶**Pair** **Read each sentence and circle the letter of the sentence that you agree with.**

1. If you have trouble working with other people, you should
   a. ask for less work.
   b. take a course or a workshop in cooperating with others.
   c. let other people have their way; don't interfere.

2. If you know what another person does well, you can
   a. try to learn new skills from that person.
   b. negotiate with that person and divide up the tasks.
   c. suggest that the other person transfer to a department where he or she will be more appreciated.

3. If you feel nervous about criticizing another person's work, you should
   a. just try to tell the truth as honestly as you can.
   b. ask sincere questions to find out why the person did what he or she did.
   c. keep your opinions to yourself; don't say anything.

◙◙ **Now listen to the cassette. Put a check (✔) next to the letter of each sentence that matches Lynn's advice. Did Lynn give Nelson the advice that you agreed with? Discuss your answers.**

2 You've got to help me get out of this mess.

▶**Pair** **Match each picture with the request for advice.**

> a. My computer crashed. You've got to help me get out of this mess.
> b. If you don't mind, I'd like to get your opinion on this project.
> c. I've tried everything, and nothing works. What do you think we should tell the customer?
> d. How can I make the graphic on this website more interesting?

"What do you mean it's not ready?"

▶**Pair** **What advice would you give Nelson in each situation? Tell the class what you would advise him to do.**

3 They'll either fix it or replace it.

Nelson is answering some messages. Complete his responses using *either . . . or*.

Incoming Messages

From: G. Day   **To:** N. Balewa

Help! My computer crashed, and when I came back from lunch it was gone! Do you know anything about this?

From: Lynn   **To:** Nelson

The old gang is getting together for dinner. Do you want to come? We were thinking Thursday, Friday, or Saturday. Which is good for you?

From: Ivan   **To:** Nelson

I called about the workshop on collaboration next week. We could drive, take the train, or go by bus. Which do you prefer?

From: D. Dahnke   **To:** N. Balewa

Has Mr. Rehan picked a name for his website yet? I thought carpets.com or rugs.com were good, but foryourfloor.com is too long, don't you think?

Outgoing Messages

From: N. Balewa   **To:** G. Day

Someone from the help desk took it. They'll either fix it or replace it.

From: Nelson   **To:** Lynn

Hi! Thanks for inviting me. I have to work Thursday night. _____

_____

From: Nelson   **To:** Ivan

I'd rather not take the bus. _____

_____

From: N. Balewa   **To:** D. Dahnke

The name rugs.com has been taken.

_____

_____

4 Career Choices

▶**Pair** Nelson is not happy with his work schedule. He's trying to decide what to do next. State his options, using the information given.

— stay here and suffer/find a new job
— take a workshop on cooperation/continue to work alone
— work constantly/take some free time
— try to control everything/find out how to learn from others
— make sure to get some exercise/live with the tension
— decide to take care of myself/feel tired all the time

Example:

Either he can stay here and suffer or he can find a new job. If he found a new job, he might have a more reasonable schedule.

▶**Class** Decide what Nelson should do and tell the class what you think.

5 I love my job!

Pair Nelson, Ivan, and Gina are attending a weekend workshop on collaboration. Look at the strengths they have listed and create sentences about their strengths using *both . . . and*.

> **Both** Ivan **and** Nelson are fast learners.
> Ivan is **both** sociable **and** reliable.

Gina	Nelson	Ivan
Strengths	**Strengths**	**Strengths**
Good at sales	Solve problems quickly	Fast learner
Good design sense	Hard worker	Reliable
Get along with coworkers	Reliable	Get along with coworkers
Flexible	Good design sense	Solve problems quickly
Ambitious	Get along well with customers	Sociable
Love my job	Fast learner	Enjoy working with others

Group Work with three other students to write sentences about characteristics that Gina, Nelson, and Ivan don't have. Begin your sentences with *neither . . . nor*. Use information from the chart above or other information you know about them.

Example:

Neither Gina nor her friends are now studying at the World Language Center.

Mixer Interview three students and ask them about their strengths. List their responses in the chart below.

(Name)	(Name)	(Name)

Pair Work with a partner to write a paragraph describing one of the students you have interviewed. Work from the notes in the chart.

Lesson 2

In this lesson, you will
- confirm information.
- make requests.
- respond to requests.

That's how it is.

Listen and read.

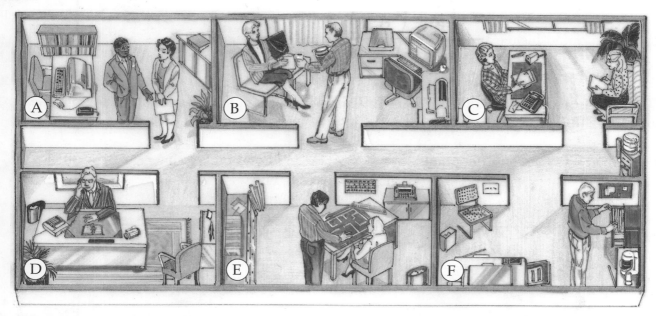

Nelson: Can I talk with you for a moment, Ms. Ho?

Ms. Ho: Make it quick, Nelson. I've got to give this report to the Sales Department by the end of the day.

Nelson: Well, it's about my work schedule. I've already worked thirty hours this week, and it's only Wednesday. I've been working most weekends, too.

Ms. Ho: I understand, Nelson. But that's how it is. We're building a new company here, and we need to be a step ahead of our competitors. If we don't give our customers excellent service, someone else will.

Nelson: Then I guess there isn't any hope of getting a fixed schedule, is there?

Ms. Ho: You'd have to work at a bigger, more established company to be able to work regular hours.

Nelson: I really like working here, though. It's exciting to design websites. And, because this is a small company, I'm getting so much opportunity to do that. But I have no time for my family and friends.

Ms. Ho: Neither of us has time for our families, Nelson. That's a choice for you to make. I can't make it for you. I can tell you this though. You're really doing great work here, and you could end up making a lot more money—we all could—if we succeed.

Pair Should Nelson stay where he is or move to a larger company? What would be the advantages and disadvantages of staying? Of going?

1 I've got to give this report to the Sales Department.

Pair Look at the office scene on page 73. Decide who is saying each statement or question and write the letter of that person's cubicle.

_____ 1. Can I help you get the report out?

_____ 2. I need to get some files for Ms. Ho.

_____ 3. Send this memo to all personnel.

_____ 4. Can I offer you some coffee?

_____ 5. Don't show these blueprints to anyone yet.

_____ 6. Could I leave a message on her voice mail?

2 I'll water them twice a week.

Pair Ms. Ho is going on a business trip and asks Nelson to do various tasks while she's away. Use the cues in the pictures to make the requests and reply to them.

A: Please water the plants for me while I'm away. **B: Of course.** I'll water them for you.	**A: Will you please show** the plans to Arthur? **B: Certainly.** I'll show them to him right away.

1. fax/estimate/new client

2. mail/letters/Mr. Burns

3. write/memo/supervisors

4. send/the announcements/all our customers

5. give/report/Beth/month's sales

6. take/packages/Kim/in shipping

Pair Ask your partner to do you a favor. Role play your exchange for the class.

Example:

A: Could you get me a piece of paper from the cabinet?

B: Sure. I'll get you two pieces.

3 I rented you a compact car.

Pair Nelson made the travel arrangements for Ms. Ho. Look at his notes and then practice a conversation like the one below.

Ms. Ho: Did you book a seat for me?

Nelson: Yes, I booked it on United Airlines.

Ms. Ho: Great!

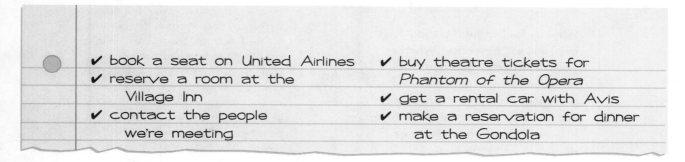

✔ book a seat on United Airlines
✔ reserve a room at the Village Inn
✔ contact the people we're meeting

✔ buy theatre tickets for *Phantom of the Opera*
✔ get a rental car with Avis
✔ make a reservation for dinner at the Gondola

4 Hi, Nelson, this is Gina.

Listen to the recorded messages that Nelson received today and the messages he left for other people. Write each caller's name and the request that was made.

5 Ad-Ons has more features than CyberWeb.

Read the advertisements for two web design companies.

AD-ONS

Why pay for features that you don't need and will never use? Whether you are just getting started or are a seasoned webmaster, most websites don't need gigabytes of disk space and 20+ e-mail accounts. Don't believe the hype—more features doesn't mean better features.

What do I get for $6.95 a month from AD-ONS?

- Home Page Development
- Informational Pages
- Interactive Pages
- Browser Compatibility INCLUDED
- Testing & Uploading INCLUDED
- Search Engine Registration FREE
- www.ownname.com
- Free Website Address
- Unlimited E-mail Forwarding
- Free Graphical Website Statistics
- Free Technical Support Via E-mail

Sign up online now

CyberWeb
Website Design

Have a product or service, but nowhere to sell it? Let the pros at CyberWeb. create a website for you. We'll build you a customized home on the Internet that you can be proud of. Take orders electronically while you sleep, build a customer base worldwide, and gain access to markets you never thought possible—all with a new website designed by CyberWeb.

CyberWeb Benefits:
- Professionally Designed Website
- Publication of the Site on the World Wide Web
- Individual Registration of Your Site with Leading Search Engines
- Free Updates to Your Site (3 per year)
- Electronic Data Gathering, E-mail Facilities, Animations, Audio, Video, and Much More
- Your Own Internet Address for Your Promotional Business Cards, Literature, Letterheads, etc.

Promote your business for just $20.00 per month on CyberWeb

Learn more, sign up today!

Group Which web design company provides better service? Make a list of the advantages and disadvantages of each one, then share your lists with the class. Use words from the box in your comparisons. Which company should Gina choose for her website?

more	fewer/less	better	worse

Example:

CyberWeb has fewer features than Ad-Ons.

In this lesson, you will
- interpret an informational article.
- discuss alternatives.

Search Engines

🔊 **Listen and read.**

Search Engines

A search engine is a computer software program that helps find information on the World Wide Web (WWW). When you use a search engine, you're asking it to look in its index to find matches with the words you type in.

Many search engines are now becoming reference sites containing much more than just search capability. They may also have news, weather, free software, picture indexes, ratings of websites, and other features.

Most engines allow you to type in a word, a phrase, or a question to find information. Chris Sherman, an authority on the Internet, suggests following these three steps to use search engines most effectively.

Before you begin your search, you should have a clear intention to either locate, browse, or consult. This will both help you to select an appropriate search tool and save a great deal of time.

Second, select the appropriate tool for your search. There are three types of search facilities available on the web: indexes, such as AltaVista and Hotbot, which are comprehensive, unstructured catalogs of just about everything published on the web; directories, like Yahoo and Excite, which are far more selective and are set up much like a library card catalog; and guides, like About.com and Look Smart, which are like online consultants, providing annotated descriptions of websites written by experts or editors.

The final step in the search process is to take a critical look at your results before you examine pages in detail. There are two key areas to look at. Titles in search results are the actual links to documents. A descriptive title can usually be one of the best indicators that you've found what you're looking for. The URL (Uniform Resource Locator—http://www.example_url.com) will also provide useful clues about a document's value. Most search engines provide both the title and the URL of a website.

Using search engines to find information can be both confusing and time-consuming. Following these three steps can make your search more fruitful. Happy searching.

Based on "Search Engines," by Chris Sherman, www.about.com

▶ **Pair** Discuss how search engines can help you with your studies. Tell the class what your thoughts are.

1 Search engines provide both news and information.

Read the article on search engines again and mark the statements _T_ (true) or _F_ (false).

_____ 1. If you want a more selective search engine, you can use either Yahoo or Excite.

_____ 2. Both Look Smart and About.com are search engines that are used as indexes.

_____ 3. Search engines can be used either to locate websites or to browse the World Wide Web.

_____ 4. Some search engines provide both search capabilities and the news.

_____ 5. Yahoo indexes the entire World Wide Web.

2 Doing a Net search can be both confusing and time-consuming.

Look at the ads and write a sentence about each one, using _both . . . and_.

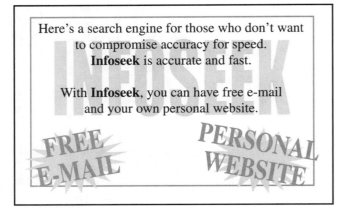

Here's a search engine for those who don't want to compromise accuracy for speed. **Infoseek** is accurate and fast.

With **Infoseek**, you can have free e-mail and your own personal website.

FREE E-MAIL   PERSONAL WEBSITE

Google
Simple and Fun
- Shop
- Chat

1.   <u>Infoseek is both fast and accurate.</u>

2. _____

_____

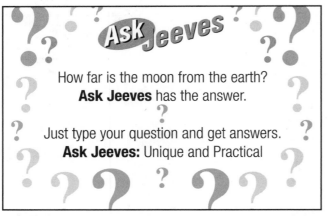

Ask Jeeves

How far is the moon from the earth?
Ask Jeeves has the answer.

Just type your question and get answers.
Ask Jeeves: Unique and Practical

alta vista
AltaVista helps you find people you lost contact with and tells you about the weather all over the world.

3. _____

_____

4. _____

_____

3 Neither Gina nor Paul is interested in camping.

For a short time, Gina has been corresponding with Paul, a man she met on the Internet. Paul has asked her to meet him, but she's not yet sure that she wants to. Read their e-mails and compare their interests, using *both . . . and* or *neither . . . nor*.

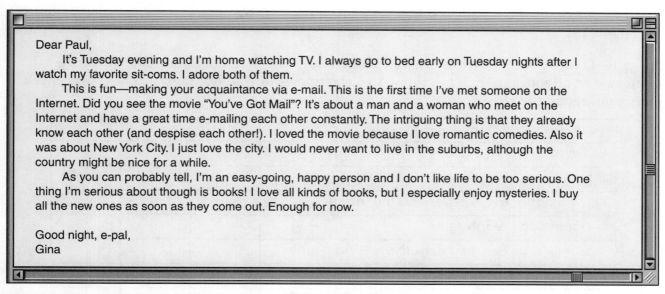

Dear Paul,

It's Tuesday evening and I'm home watching TV. I always go to bed early on Tuesday nights after I watch my favorite sit-coms. I adore both of them.

This is fun—making your acquaintance via e-mail. This is the first time I've met someone on the Internet. Did you see the movie "You've Got Mail"? It's about a man and a woman who meet on the Internet and have a great time e-mailing each other constantly. The intriguing thing is that they already know each other (and despise each other!). I loved the movie because I love romantic comedies. Also it was about New York City. I just love the city. I would never want to live in the suburbs, although the country might be nice for a while.

As you can probably tell, I'm an easy-going, happy person and I don't like life to be too serious. One thing I'm serious about though is books! I love all kinds of books, but I especially enjoy mysteries. I buy all the new ones as soon as they come out. Enough for now.

Good night, e-pal,
Gina

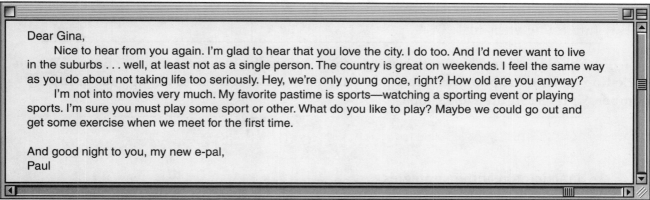

Dear Gina,

Nice to hear from you again. I'm glad to hear that you love the city. I do too. And I'd never want to live in the suburbs . . . well, at least not as a single person. The country is great on weekends. I feel the same way as you do about not taking life too seriously. Hey, we're only young once, right? How old are you anyway?

I'm not into movies very much. My favorite pastime is sports—watching a sporting event or playing sports. I'm sure you must play some sport or other. What do you like to play? Maybe we could go out and get some exercise when we meet for the first time.

And good night to you, my new e-pal,
Paul

▶**Class** Do you think Paul is a good match for Gina? Do you think they'd get along well together? Why or why not? Write a short e-mail response from Gina to Paul.

4 Online

Log onto http://www.prenhall.com/brown_activities
The Web: Searching for Information
Grammar: What's your grammar IQ?
E-mail: Did You Know?

5 Wrap Up

▶**Group** Look at the following Internet workshops. Check (✔) the ones you would be interested in attending. Then interview two classmates to find out their interests and check their answers on the chart.

Internet workshops	You		
Learn more about e-mail			
Internet as a research tool			
Downloading free software on the Internet			
Shopping on the Internet			
Internet: Your personal detective to find people			
Playing games on the Internet: Learn the rules			
Trading stocks on the Internet			
Interesting websites			

▶**Group** Share your answers with your group. Discuss the reasons for your choices. Which workshop is the most popular? Least popular? Then write sentences about your group members' interest in the workshops.

Strategies for Success

➤ Practicing reading strategies
➤ Planning listening strategies
➤ Giving advice and opinions

1. Look for an article in a magazine, newspaper, or on the internet that interests you. Practice the following reading strategies with the article: 1. Scan for the main idea. 2. Skim it for the general overall meaning, or "gist." 3. Read the article. 4. As you read, highlight or underline any words you don't know, then guess their meaning from context.

2. In your journal for this unit, think of goals that you can set for doing more *listening* to English. List those goals specifically (for example, "I will listen to (and watch) English-speaking TV for two hours this week.")

3. With a partner, look in an English-speaking magazine or newspaper for advertisements for either (a) mobile phone service, (b) travel package, or (c) an automobile. Choose one, and give opinions to your partner on the advantages and disadvantages of the product or service. Practice the language you learned in this unit for interpreting information and giving advice.

CHECKPOINT

How much have you learned in this unit? Review the goals for each lesson. What skills can you confidently use now? What skills do you need to practice? List these below.

Skills I've Learned Well

_____

_____

_____

_____

Skills I Need to Practice

_____

_____

_____

_____

Learning Preferences

In this unit, which type of activity did you like the best and the least? Write the number in the box: 1 = best; 2 = next best; 3 = next; 4 = least.

❏ Working by myself   ❏ Working with a group

❏ Working with a partner   ❏ Working as a whole class

In this unit, which exercises helped you to learn to:

listen more effectively?   Exercise _____   read more easily?   Exercise _____

speak more fluently?   Exercise _____   write more clearly? Exercise _____

Which exercise did you like the most? _____   Why? _____

Which exercise did you like the least? _____   Why? _____

Vocabulary

Verbs
book
browse
consult
crash
interfere
negotiate
replace
trade

Nouns
announcement
estimate
fax
feature
search engine
shipping
software
stocks
tool
workshop

Expressions
get out of (a mess)
in the long run
invest energy in

Adjectives
flexible
incompetent/competent
reliable
selective

GRAMMAR SUMMARY

Either . . . or

The meeting was **either** postponed **or** canceled.
Either he can stay and suffer **or** he can find a new job.

Both . . . and

Both Ivan **and** Nelson are fast learners.

Neither . . . nor

Neither Gina nor her friends are now studying at the World Language Center.

Direct and indirect objects

Please **write** a memo **to the supervisors**.
I'll **write them** a memo immediately.

Did you **book** a seat **for me**?
Yes, I **booked** it on United Airlines.

Comparison of nouns

Ad-Ons has **more** features **than** CyberWeb.
CyberWeb has **fewer** features **than** Ad-Ons.

COMMUNICATION SUMMARY

Talking about conditions

If you work late too often, you should do some work on your schedule.

Asking for advice

You've got to help me get out of this mess.
I'd like to get your opinion on this project.

Giving advice

If you know what the other person does well, you can negotiate with that person and divide up the tasks.

Confirming information

Did you book a seat for me?
Yes, I booked it on United Airlines.

Making requests

Please water the plants for me while I'm away.

Responding to requests

Of course, I'll water them for you.

Discussing alternatives

Either he can stay here and suffer or he can find a new job.
Neither Gina nor Paul is interested in camping.

UNIT 7

Lesson 1

In this lesson, you will

- talk about plans.
- follow technical directions.
- state technical information.
- describe likes and dislikes.

Planning a Visit

🔊 **Ivan and Nelson are going to visit Pablo at the Sterling Flight Center Aviation School in south Florida. Read and listen to Pablo's e-mail to Nelson.**

From:	Pablo.Bonilla@www.com
Sent:	Tuesday, March 5, 2000 4:28 P.M.
To:	Nelson.Balewa@aol.com
Subject:	Vacation Plans

Hi Nelson,

I'm really looking forward to seeing you and Ivan next week. Since you want me to plan the visit, here's what I have in mind. On Thursday, I've asked my flight instructor to show you our flight simulator. You'll really seem to take off and make adjustments to speed and altitude.

Then, on Friday, we'll grab our sleeping bags and head out to a river or lake somewhere and kick back and listen to the sounds of nature. Tell Ivan to bring along his fishing pole and we can catch ourselves some supper. Saturday, we can take a walk on the wild side at Lion Country Safari, which is the nation's first drive-through "cageless" zoo. The Safari invites us to drive past more than a thousand animals from around the world, and they expect us to give the animals the right of way!

On Sunday, if you don't mind a long ride, we can visit the National Archaeological Park in St. Augustine, the oldest historic site in the United States. We can even drink from the prehistoric Indian Spring that Ponce de Leon hoped was the Fountain of Youth. Oh, and Ivan wanted me to get tickets for a baseball game, but the season hasn't officially begun yet. Tell him to let me know if he wants to see an exhibition game, though.

I'll pick you up at the airport on Wednesday, the 13th, at 9:00. See you then.

▶ **Pair** **What are some popular vacation places in your country? If friends came to visit you, where would you take them?**

1 Ready for Take-off

Pablo's flight instructor is showing Nelson and Ivan how to make a simulated take-off. Listen and complete the chart as he gives them instructions.

When	What	How
1. Ready for take-off	• Check that the parking brake is set • Apply full throttle • Release the parking brake	• Press _____F4_____ • Wait for engines to build up thrust and press _____
2. Speed is _____ knots	• Start plane rising	• Pull back the joystick very gently until _____ of plane rises
3. During manual climb	• Ensure speed of plane is _____ _____	• Push the joystick a bit _____
4. When airborne	• Gear up	• Press _____
5. Speed is at least 190 knots	• Retract flaps • Activate autopilot	• Press _____ • Press controls _____, _ALT_, _A/T arm_.
6. Autopilot controls plane	• Ascend to altitude of _____ feet.	• Climb _____ feet per minute

2 He advised them to check the parking brake.

Pair Look at the chart above and talk about the directions the flight instructor gave Ivan and Nelson. Use verbs from the box below.

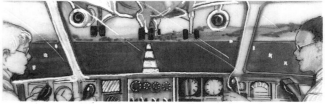

ask	expect	get	need	promise	want
cause	forbid	help	order	remind	warn
encourage	force	invite	persuade	teach	would like

He	advised allowed	them	to check to activate	the parking brake. the autopilot.

Now answer questions about your English teacher.

1. What does he or she encourage you to do?
2. How does he or she help you to do that?
3. Is there anything that he or she doesn't allow you to do? Why?
4. What does he or she advise you to do? Why?
5. Would you prefer to do something other than what your teacher expects?

Class Report your discussions to the class.

3 Experience the adventure.

▶ **Group** Ivan wants to visit Lion Country Safari, but Nelson feels like going to St. Augustine. Read the ads below and answer the questions that follow.

Your Passport to 500 Wild Acres of Animals, Rides, Games & Thrills

As America's first drive-through "cageless" zoo, Lion Country Safari has been a leader in conservation since 1967. Lion Country provides a habitat in which many endangered or threatened species live and reproduce. Drive through our cageless zoo and encounter all of the magnificent animals we have to offer.

In the Nature Walk, visitors walk into the aviary, where beautiful, friendly parrots will fly over to you and allow you to feed them. Safari World also features a squirrel monkey exhibit. On islands in Lake Shanalee, visitors will notice a family of siamangs and a group of spider monkeys.

Across from the Petting Zoo is the Alligator moat, where our American alligators are kept. Alligator Chit-Chat takes place every day at 3:00 P.M., when one of our knowledgeable staff members shares information about these animals while feeding them.

St. Augustine Great Getaway

St Augustine, the oldest European settlement in the United States, was founded in 1565 by the Spanish explorer Pedro Menendez de Aviles.

There's a wonderful sense of antiquity to be found here, and there's a lot to see and do. Fascinating walking tours of the Oldest City, led by guides in period costume, take you down the narrow streets. These are treasure troves of beautifully preserved historical sites, tracing American history back to its earliest days. Here you can find the oldest house, the oldest wooden schoolhouse, and the oldest masonry fort in the United States. Narrated sightseeing tours are also available on delightful open-air trolleys or antique trains and horse-drawn carriages, and cruises are available on scenic Matanzas Bay.

Of course, any mention of St. Augustine must include the quest for the "fountain of youth." Discovered by Ponce de Leon in 1513, the Fountain of Youth contains foundations and artifacts from the first mission and colony.

Source: http://www.lioncountrysafari.com

Lion Country Safari

1. Why is Lion Country Safari considered a leader in conservation?
2. What does Lion Country keep providing?
3. What do the parrots enjoy doing?
4. What do visitors expect to see on the islands?
5. What do staff members arrange to do every day at 3:00 P.M.?

Source: http://www.funandsun.com

St. Augustine

1. Why does the ad recommend visiting St. Augustine?
2. What can visitors hope to find there?
3. What do walking tours promise to include?
4. What can visitors look forward to seeing?
5. What can visitors to the Fountain of Youth expect to see?

▶ **Class** Ponce de Leon spent his life in search of the Fountain of Youth. Supposedly the water from this mythical fountain would allow a person to live forever. If you had the chance to live forever, would you take it? Discuss your reasons.

4 Volunteers Invited to Chimps' Birthday Party

▶**Pair** Complete the press release with the appropriate form (infinitive or gerund) of the verbs in parentheses.

**Volunteers Are Invited to Attend Chimps'
Birthday Party
October 20
For Immediate Release**

What's more exciting than a birthday party for one-year-old twins, chimp twins at that? Who wouldn't enjoy _____ time out of a busy schedule to *(1. take)* visit the chimps at world-famous Lion Country Safari, especially for a birthday party? All the volunteers who have worked on the chimp islands have been invited _____ the birthday festivities. They have *(2. attend)* been asked _____ wrapped presents—stuffed *(3. bring)* animals, balls, and fruit—for the chimps to have fun unwrapping them. There will be two big birthday cakes, one for all the chimps and one for their human friends.

Chimpanzees by nature are very curious and very intelligent animals, and they need _____ *(4. have)* daily stimulation. Who can resist _____ them *(5. provide)* with stimulating new toys to enrich their environment? Not the volunteers who are planning _____ *(6. buy)* lots of toys for their friends!

The volunteers are recruited _____ *(7. assist)* with a research project, developed by renowned chimpanzee expert Jane Goodall. Ms. Goodall has called Lion Country Safari's chimpanzee display the largest in North America, and she says it is the finest display in the world, outside of Africa.

▶**Group** Discuss this story. What do you think about bringing birthday gifts to the chimpanzees? Do you think this is a good thing to do? Report the group's opinions to the class.

5 I enjoy visiting theme parks, but Maria can't stand them.

Complete the questionnaire. Use the key to mark your likes and dislikes.

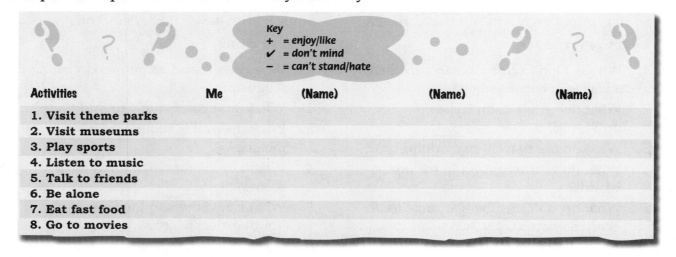

Key
+ = *enjoy/like*
✔ = *don't mind*
– = *can't stand/hate*

Activities	Me	(Name)	(Name)	(Name)
1. Visit theme parks				
2. Visit museums				
3. Play sports				
4. Listen to music				
5. Talk to friends				
6. Be alone				
7. Eat fast food				
8. Go to movies				

▶**Mixer** Interview three classmates and fill in their attitudes on the chart. Report your findings to the class.

Lesson 2

In this lesson, you will
- talk about ambitions.
- talk about sequence of events.

Lifelong Learning

Listen and read.

Gina: I'm exhausted. Working during the day and taking classes in the evening is tough.

Lynn: Tell me about it. After working all day long, I just want to come home and crash. I'm exhausted. You know what's funny though . . . I have classmates who could be my grandparents, and they're full of energy.

Gina: Me too. One of the students in my class is over 60, and she's so motivated.

Lynn: Why do you think someone at that age would go back to school?

Gina: I asked Melinda, my classmate, the same question. She said she always wanted to study fashion, so after retiring from her job, she went back to school.

Lynn: Personally, I'd rather spend time with my grandchildren after I retire.

Gina: I guess lifelong learning has become an American phenomenon. As far as I know, there are only a few countries where there's no age restriction for attending college.

Lynn: I think it's great to have senior citizens sitting in the same class with younger students. It benefits both.

Gina: I agree. I really feel inspired by students like Melinda. When I'm talking to her, I feel her passion for learning and her determination to get another degree.

Lynn: And I think they find it stimulating to be around younger students too.

Gina: Yes, especially when we have class discussions. And, having a lot of life experience and a different perspective, they can teach us a lot.

Lynn: I'm sure our professors love to have senior citizens in their classes. I would if I were a teacher.

Gina: Me too.

Pair An 80-year-old American woman graduated from college in May 2000. What do you think of this phenomenon of lifelong learning?

1 After graduating from college, Gina is going to open her own business.

▶**Pair** Look at the flowchart and discuss Gina's plans for the future. Then write a paragraph describing her plans, beginning with the sentence below.

After graduating from college, Gina is going to open her own business.

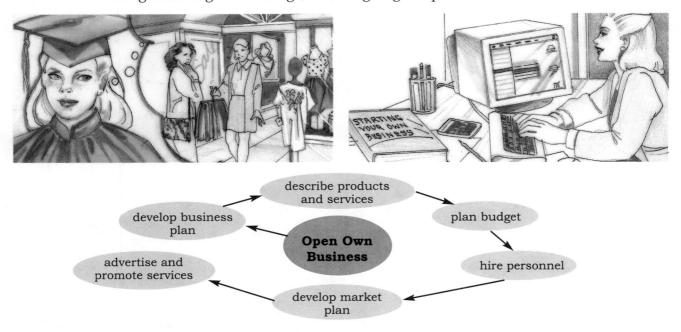

Decide on a goal that you want to achieve. Create a flowchart like Gina's that illustrates the steps you need to take to achieve your goal. Present your flowchart to the class.

2 Before starting out, list your reasons for wanting to go into business.

Gina is taking a course on "How to Start a Small Business." Listen to the instructor's advice and check the items that contain that same advice.

_____ 1. Before opening a business, you should do the necessary research and planning.

_____ 2. Before starting out, make a list of your reasons for wanting to go into business.

_____ 3. When determining what business is right for you, you should ignore your hobbies and interests.

_____ 4. When identifying the role your business will play, you should check out the competition.

_____ 5. To create a demand for your business, you should take out expensive newspaper ads.

_____ 6. As you develop your plan, you should consult a pre-business checklist.

_____ 7. After creating a business plan, you don't have to worry about how the business will be operated, managed, and financed.

Source: http://www.sba.gov/starting/indexsteps.html

3 Lynn's schedule is very busy.

▶ **Pair** **Read an e-mail from Lynn to Tony and Oscar. Then rewrite the numbered clauses as** *–ing* **phrases on the lines.**

I've had a hectic life **since I started** college a couple of months ago. I've had a hectic life **since starting** college a couple of months ago.	**Since I started** college a couple of months ago, I've had a hectic life. **Since starting** college a couple of months ago, I've had a hectic life.

Hi,

    I'm sorry I haven't been able to e-mail you for a while. I've had a hectic life **(1) since I started** college a couple of months ago. I've never been so busy in my life. **(2) After I get up** in the morning, I review my notes from the previous night. I usually work from 8:00 to 5:00, unless I'm on a night shift, which is rare because of my classes. Most of my classes are after 5:00, so **(3) after I get off** work, I take the bus to school. I'm so tired that sometimes in class while I'm supposed to be listening to the instructor, I doze off. **(4) When I arrive** home, I crash on the couch. **(5) Before I make** dinner, I take a short nap. **(6) After I clean** the kitchen and **wash the dishes**, I study until at least 1 o'clock in the morning.

    Enough complaining. By the way, Oscar, would you send me that recipe you mentioned in one of your e-mails?

Lynn

1. _____.

2. _____.

3. _____.

4. _____.

5. _____.

6. _____.

4 Before going to the interview, I'd rehearse my responses.

▶ **Pair** **Discuss what you would do** *before* **and** *after* **each activity.**

1. You have a job interview tomorrow.
   Before going to the interview, I'd rehearse responses to possible questions with a friend. After finishing the interview, I'd write down the highlights of the conversation I want to remember.

2. You're driving down the highway and you get a flat tire. You have to change it.

3. You're giving a party for a friend's birthday.

4. You need to write a term paper for one of your classes.

5. You decide to paint a room that has old wallpaper on the walls.

5 After boiling the water, add rice to it.

Pair Read Oscar's e-mail response to Lynn. Rewrite his recipe in paragraph form, using *before, after, while* and the *–ing* form of the verbs.

1. Heat 3 tablespoons of oil in a nonstick pan and sauté a pound of chicken legs or breasts over medium heat. Stir occasionally with a wooden spoon for 20 minutes.

2. Add a teaspoon of salt, pepper, and turmeric, and 6 pounds of chopped spinach, and cover and cook for 10 minutes over medium heat.

3. Add 3 cups of pitted prunes, 1 cup of water, and 3 tablespoons of orange juice; cover and simmer for about an hour longer over low heat.

4. Check to see that the chicken is cooked, then transfer the stew into a deep casserole. Cover and place in a warm oven until ready to serve.

5. Serve the chicken hot from the same dish with saffron rice.

Group Bring your favorite recipe to class and teach it to a partner or the whole class. Describe the steps involved in preparing it.

Lesson 3

In this lesson, you will
- discuss quality.
- describe recent experiences.

Work in the 21st Century

 Listen and read.

A New Model for Workplace Effectiveness
by Vivian Bradshaw

A new model of management has been slowly spreading throughout the corporate world. Called workplace synergy, it marks a shift away from the old model of competition among employees to an emphasis on developing systems that reward cooperation.

There are on-the-job workshops and training sessions on self-awareness and listening to and valuing others' point of view. Whereas once managers ruled by the fear principle, "Work harder than the next guy or lose that promotion," they now try to foster a "one for all, and all for one" way of thinking.

"We recognized that competitive models did not do a thing for our productivity. Instead, they created unnecessary tension in relationships among people who needed to work with each other," says Sara Cohen, who oversees an advertising agency in downtown Cincinnati.

The changes are evident from the moment one steps off the elevator on the 14th floor of a downtown office building. Overstuffed couches, plants, and rustic wooden tables give the work areas a homelike feel. Walls and partitions have been redesigned to allow for community as well as privacy, and it is possible to see clusters of people talking and laughing around an espresso machine.

Changing the atmosphere is only one aspect of workplace synergy. At Cartwright and Wiseman, a San Francisco investment firm, Carol Stephanopolis-Schmidt recently led employees through a workshop where they identified their personality types. "We find that after the training, people not only become more tolerant of one another's differences, but they begin to see how different preferences might benefit them," she says. "You find out that the other guy wants to do the part of the project that you dread, and suddenly it all makes sense."

The hardest part is getting people to stop trying to change other people. "Someone is always asking me for advice on getting a coworker to be more flexible, but that's the wrong approach. You can't do anything about the other guy. What you can do is work on yourself and developing your understanding."

▶ **Class** Is workplace synergy better than a traditional work environment? On the board, make a list of the advantages and disadvantages of a cooperative work environment.

UNIT 7 91

1 It's possible to see employees joking and laughing.

Read the following sentences and mark WS if it describes workplace synergy or T if it represents a more traditional workplace atmosphere.

_____ 1. It's possible to see employees joking and laughing in the halls.

_____ 2. The walls are decorated with photographs of the founders of the company.

_____ 3. Senior executives always wear suits to work.

_____ 4. On Fridays, it's common for employees to wear jeans to work.

_____ 5. Mangers often ask for employee input when making decisions.

_____ 6. Managers make all decisions regarding employee affairs.

_____ 7. Employees maintain a cooperative spirit when solving problems.

_____ 8. Employees turn to the manager for help when facing a problem.

2 I buy casual clothes when shopping for work clothes.

▶Pair Look at the pictures and discuss the management styles of Sam Farrell and Paula Cooper. Then complete their conversation with an *–ing* verb phrase.

Sam Farrell: Our employees come to work **wearing conservative clothes**.

Paula Cooper: At our company, employees can show up **wearing anything that is comfortable**.

Sam Farrell: I do my best work sitting alone in my office.

Paula Cooper: Really? Not me. I do my best work _____.

Sam Farrell: Well, my employees spend much of their time working at computer terminals.

Paula Cooper: I see. People at our company spend a lot of their time _____ _____.

Sam Farrell: That's odd. Our employees would have a hard time working in groups.

Paula Cooper: I guess there are many ways to run an office. In our office, it is common to see the staff _____.

Sam Farrell: Well, I guess I'm happy right where I am,

_____.

▶Pair Which office would you be more comfortable working in? Why? Share your opinions with the class.

3 I'd like to find work helping people.

Check three items that describe the type of job you would prefer to have.

✔ **Interest Survey**

I would prefer a job
_____ using technology
_____ designing things
_____ helping people
_____ working outdoors

_____ requiring interaction with others
_____ requiring leadership skills
_____ requiring verbal skills
_____ requiring creativity

Pair Ask and answer questions about the kind of work your partner prefers. Discuss the possible jobs that might fit your preferences.

Are you interested in a job **using technology**?	Yes, I would like a job **working with speech-recognition devices**.
Would you like a job **designing software**?	Yes, I would.
	Well, I would prefer to find work **editing movies**.

4 I have just been to the worst workshop of my life.

Pair Gina, Lynn, and Ivan are discussing their on-the-job training workshops over dinner. Which one was the worst in your opinion?

Gina: I've just finished a makeup workshop, and all the woman did was talk! She said she had forgotten to bring her makeup. Can you imagine that? Ridiculous! Of course, it was impossible to learn anything. I didn't want to be antisocial, so I stayed, but I wanted to leave.

Lynn: I had an unbearable experience at a workshop too. I went to a workshop on retirement planning. The woman in charge was incapable of keeping her notes straight, so she spent half the day retelling what she had already told us.

Ivan: That's pretty bad, but I went to a workshop that disappeared. It had been scheduled for a Saturday morning from 8:00 to 12:00. I got up and dragged myself in—and guess what? It had been canceled! How's that for an irresponsible work ethic?

Class Find the words in the discussion above that have the following meanings.

1. The opposite of responsible
2. The opposite of social
3. The opposite of appear
4. The opposite of possible
5. The opposite of bearable
6. The opposite of capable

Group Think of a bad experience you have had. Describe your experience to the group, using some of the prefixes above.

5 Online

Log onto http://www.prenhall.com/brown_activities
The Web: Theme Parks
Grammar: What's your grammar IQ?
E-mail: In My Free Time

6 Wrap Up

▶Group **Plan a workshop to present to your classmates. Follow the instructions below.**

1. Choose a topic for the workshop from the list or use your own idea.

    - Developing good study skills
    - Memorizing new vocabulary
    - Making friends

    - Planning a vacation
    - Getting a good job
    - Improving your home

2. Decide what the participants need to know about your topic and write an introduction.

3. Plan an activity that the participants can do in your workshop and gather any materials you need.

4. Make a schedule for your workshop.

5. Decide what each member of your group will be responsible for.

6. Decide on any comments that you want to make at the end. Also think about asking participants for feedback on their experience.

7. Present your workshop!

Strategies for Success

- ➤ **Using language to plan, express desires, and negotiate agreement**
- ➤ **Planning speaking strategies**
- ➤ **Talking about career hopes and plans**

1. First with a partner, then with the whole class, plan a field trip to a museum, park, or other point of interest. Make sure you say what your desires are ("I hope to go to the park.") and make recommendations ("I recommend going to the art museum.") Also, describe your likes and dislikes and then come to an agreement on where to go and other plans.

2. In your journal for this unit, think of goals that you can set for doing more *speaking* in English. List those goals specifically (for example, "I will speak with a native English speaker for one hour this week.")

3. With a partner, talk about your career hopes and plans. Make sure you use the future tense and express your preferences. ("I am going to apply for graduate school." "I would prefer a job that pays lots of money.")

CHECKPOINT

How much have you learned in this unit? Review the goals for each lesson. What skills can you confidently use now? What skills do you need to practice? List these below.

Skills I've Learned Well

_____

_____

_____

_____

Skills I Need to Practice

_____

_____

_____

_____

Learning Preferences

In this unit, which type of activity did you like the best and the least? Write the number in the box: 1 = best; 2 = next best; 3 = next; 4 = least.

❑ Working by myself   ❑ Working with a group

❑ Working with a partner   ❑ Working as a whole class

In this unit, which exercises helped you to learn to:

listen more effectively?   Exercise _____   read more easily?   Exercise _____

speak more fluently?   Exercise _____   write more clearly?   Exercise _____

Which exercise did you like the most? _____   Why? _____

Which exercise did you like the least? _____ Why? _____

Vocabulary

Verbs	Nouns	Adjectives
advertise	competition	[anti]social
cause	creativity	casual
encourage	device	conservative
expect		[dis]appeared
forbid		effective
force		hectic
order		[im]possible
persuade		[in]capable
promise		[ir]responsible
promote		motivated
rehearse		tolerant
remind		[un]bearable
warn		

Verb + direct object + infinitive

He **advised them to check** the parking brake.

Common verbs in this pattern:

ask	expect	get	need	promise	want
cause	forbid	help	order	remind	warn
encourage	force	invite	persuade	teach	would like

Review: Verb + infinitive (*to* + verb)

Ivan **wants to go** to Lion Country Safari.

Common verbs in this pattern:

agree	expect	offer	refuse
appear	hope	plan	seem
arrange	intend	pretend	want
can afford	need	promise	would like

Verb + gerund (verb + *-ing*)

Nelson **recommends going** to St. Augustine.

Common verbs in this pattern:

appreciate	enjoy	postpone
avoid	finish	practice
consider	keep [on]	recommend
discuss	look forward to	resist

Review: Verb + either infinitive or gerund

What do you **like to do** in your free time?
What do you **like doing** in your free time?

Common verbs in this pattern:

begin	can't stand	continue	like
love	prefer	stop	try

Prefixes im-, in-, un-, ir-, anti-, dis-

antisocial	incapable
disappeared	irresponsible
impossible	unbearable

Participles in adverbial phrases

After graduating from college, Gina is going to open a business.

Participles in adjective phrases

It's possible to see employees **laughing** and **joking** in the halls.

Talking about plans

Sunday we can visit the National Archaeological Park.

Following technical directions

Ascend to altitude of 12,500 feet.

Stating technical information

He advised them to check the parking brake.

Describing likes and dislikes

I enjoy visiting theme parks, but Maria can't stand them.

Talking about ambitions

After graduating from college, Gina is going to open a business.

Talking about sequence of events

After working all day, I just want to come home and crash.

Discussing quality

I do my best work sitting alone in my office.

Describing recent experiences

I had an unbearable experience at a workshop too.

UNIT 8

Lesson 1

In this lesson, you will

- talk about changes.
- state rules.
- express hope.
- speculate about the future.

Advancement in the Workplace

🔊 **Listen and read.**

Gina: So what's the exciting news, Nelson?

Ivan: Are you getting married?

Nelson: No, not yet. The news is that . . . I was promoted. Now I'm leading the design team at my company.

Sofia: That's great. Congratulations.

Ivan: Does it mean more money as well as more work?

Nelson: Well, I've already been given more responsibilities, but we haven't talked about the raise yet.

Gina: You're working very hard there. I'm sure you'll get a good raise.

Nelson: Yes, and I should get it soon. I owe this promotion in part to Ms. Ho, my boss. She's not only supported my growth in the company, but she's also been a mentor for me.

Sofia: What do you mean?

Nelson: I mean I've learned a lot from her diligence and responsibility and her ability to balance work and leisure. In fact, she was promoted to a higher management position because of her hard work.

Ivan: How about a company car? I hope you get one.

Gina: Ivan, stop it!

Nelson: I don't know. Maybe if I need to travel on business . . .

Ivan: And an office to yourself.

Nelson: Actually, yes. I'm getting Ms. Ho's office.

Gina: I'm really happy for you, Nelson. We all are. You really deserve it.

Nelson: Thank you. I feel very lucky right now, having friends like you and a job I love—even though it makes me crazy sometimes.

▶ **Pair** Why did Nelson and Ms. Ho get promoted? Discuss other reasons people are promoted.

1 Nelson will be given a raise soon.

Read the statements about Nelson's promotion and check (✔) the ones that are true.

____ 1. He will be given an office.

____ 2. He will be given a company car.

____ 3. He is going to be awarded a college scholarship.

____ 4. He will be offered stock options in his company.

____ 5. He will be given a raise soon.

____ 6. He may be sent on more business trips.

2 Many changes will be made under Nelson's leadership.

🔊 **Listen as Nelson tells his team about the changes he foresees in the company. Then write a sentence briefly explaining what he said about each of the following.**

1. customers _Customers should be given quality service._

2. responsibilities _____

3. weekly meetings _____

4. suggestions _____

5. bonuses _____

6. annual meetings _____

7. travel expenses _____

8. casual clothes _____

▶**Pair** **How would you react to these changes if you worked on Nelson's team? Why?**

3 No children are allowed at work.

Group Read the memo from Nelson about the company's policies and rules. Then discuss the regulations. Are they fair? Are there any you disagree with?

Memo

Dear Colleagues,

Since I assumed responsibility as the new website development leader, I've been asked time and again whether there will be changes in workplace rules and policies. Although most of the policies and procedures will be unchanged, I am making the following changes:

1. In the past, some employees have brought their children to work. This has been disturbing to some colleagues and has disrupted their work. Therefore, no children are allowed in the office from now on. Other arrangements for children should be made.

2. Some employees have been seen using the copy machine for personal purposes. Please keep in mind that the copy machine must be used only for work-related jobs.

3. The Internet and e-mail are major tools in our work. They should not be used for personal reasons.

4. Some employees have been coming to work in shorts. Although casual clothes are fine, shorts and tank tops are not permitted.

5. Finally, for vacations longer than 3 days, notification two weeks in advance is required.

Pair What are some of the rules and policies at your school? Make a list of the rules and share them with the class.

4 Something has to be done!

Pair Read what's happening at Nelson's company. Then state how Nelson hopes to change things for the better.

> Nelson hopes (that) he can make some improvements.
> Nelson hopes to make some improvements.

1. An employee uses the company phone to make personal long-distance calls all the time.
   <u>Nelson hopes (that) he can stop these personal calls.</u>

2. Two employees are always arguing with each other.
   _____

3. Some employees call in sick at least once a week.
   _____

4. Some employees download software programs off the company computer.
   _____

5. Some employees come in to work late almost every day.
   _____

5 A Party for Nelson

🔊 Sofia, Ivan, and Gina are planning on throwing a party to celebrate Nelson's recent promotion. Listen and make a list of what will be done in preparation.

1.   _The food will be catered._ .
2.   _____ .
3.   _____ .
4.   _____ .

▶**Group** Make a list of reasons people have parties. Rank the occasions in order of importance in people's lives. Discuss your list with the class.

6 Let's speculate about the future.

Nelson and his team are working on a website that speculates about the next 50 years. Look at their survey posted on the website and check (✔) whether you agree or disagree with the speculations.

Speculations	Agree	Disagree
1. Almost all work will be done at home via the Internet.		
2. Children will have robots as their babysitters.		
3. Cars will be made smaller to save energy and protect the environment.		
4. Cures will be discovered for AIDS and cancer.		
5. A woman will be elected president of the United States.		
6. Schools could be abolished because students will be taught via the Internet.		
7. Traveling might be done in a virtual world created by computers.		
8. Learning another language won't be considered necessary because computers will be able to translate simultaneously.		
9. (Your own idea) _____		

▶**Class** Discuss your views about the future.

In this lesson, you will
- draw conclusions.
- express and respond to anger.
- persuade someone not to act impulsively.

- talk about past advisability.
- talk about possibilities.

I'm just beginning to learn how things work.

Listen and read.

Ms. Pavlik: What's the matter, Nelson? Don't you like this place?

Nelson: Oh, yeah . . . um . . . I love it.

Ms. Pavlik: Nelson, you seem distracted. If it's about the website, I cleared the changes. Tyler shouldn't have suggested all those bells and whistles. We're going clean and simple as you suggested.

Nelson: Uh-huh.

Ms. Pavlik: Nelson, are you here with me today?

Nelson: Oh, I'm sorry. I wasn't listening. But, Ms. Pavlik, I wouldn't dream of bothering you with my problems. I promise, I'll concentrate on the project.

Ms. Pavlik: Oh, I'm tired of talking business. Tell me what's on your mind. I love to talk about personal problems. And, please, call me Anna.

Nelson: How do you know it's a personal problem? Anyway, I don't want to complain.

Ms. Pavlik: Go ahead, tell me.

Nelson: I feel kind of embarrassed talking to a client, but I just got a promotion to team leader, and now one of my colleagues is giving me a hard time. I'm wondering if I could have done something wrong. But don't worry. It won't interfere with our work.

Ms. Pavlik: Ahhhh, don't worry about it. Come on, our table is ready. Let's go sit down and you can tell me about this coworker of yours. I'm an expert in office politics.

Nelson: And I'm just beginning to learn how things work.

▶ **Group** Is it appropriate to talk to a customer about a problem with a coworker? Why or why not?

1 She refused to speak to me.

Pair Nelson is complaining about his problems with a coworker. Express your conclusions and advice using *would have, could have, should have, may have, might have,* and *must have* to express conclusions and advice.

> I said hello to Paula at the coffee machine, but she didn't answer.
> Conclusion: She **might not have heard**.
> Advice: You **should have spoken** louder.

1. Paula didn't come to the meeting.

Conclusion: _____

Advice: _____

2. Paula didn't respond to my message.

Conclusion: _____

Advice: _____

3. Paula took important disks from my desk without asking me.

Conclusion: _____

Advice: _____

4. Paula yelled at me in front of the team.

Conclusion: _____

Advice: _____

Group What conclusions can you draw about Nelson's relationship with Paula? Have you ever had a problem like this with a coworker or a classmate? Tell the group about it.

2 Take it easy.

Pair Discuss the expressions and write a dialog for one of the two situations shown.

Expressing anger	Responding to anger
This is ridiculous!	It's OK. Calm down.
I've had it with him (her)!	Take it easy.
I'm fed up with this project.	It'll work out. Try to see it through.
I'm losing my temper.	You need to cool off.

Class Role play your dialog for the class.

3 You're late!

▶**Group** How would you persuade the following people not to act impulsively?

1. Paula

2. Nelson

3. Ms. Pavlik

Nelson is always on my back at work. He's such a perfectionist. It's getting ridiculous. I feel like quitting my job.

I'm fed up. Paula is stubborn and rude. She doesn't cooperate. I'm going to ask to work with someone else on this project.

My partner always wants to discuss things after decisions have been made. I feel like telling him not to waste our time.

4 I should have told you about my problems.

🔘 Listen to the conversation between Nelson and Paula. Check (✔) the name of the person who has drawn each of the conclusions.

	Nelson	Paula
My coworker doesn't like me.		
My coworker isn't a good team player.		
My coworker is never happy with my work.		
My coworker is jealous of me.		
My coworker is rude.		

▶**Class** Listen to the conversation again. Which of Nelson's and Paula's conclusions were correct?

5 If Anna hasn't come yet, the meeting may have lasted longer than expected.

▶ **Pair** Nelson and Paula had **an appointment** with Anna Pavlik, but she didn't show up. Nelson got upset. What *may/might have* happened?

1. If Anna wasn't feeling well, _____

2. If Anna was going to be late, _____

3. If Anna got stuck in a meeting, _____

4. If Anna's partner needed her help, _____

▶ **Pair** Have you ever had to wait for someone who didn't show up? What did you do?

6 I've tried to understand what caused the conflict.

Check (✔) the things that you have done when you were angry with someone. Cross out the things you have never done. Then add other things you have done to the list.

_____ I've argued with the person.

_____ I've stopped talking to the person.

_____ I've said things that I regretted later.

_____ I've taken time to cool off and think about the issue more calmly.

_____ I've tried to understand what caused the conflict.

· _____ I've tried to understand the other person's point of view.

_____ I've evaluated my reasons for being angry.

_____ I've apologized.

Other things you have done:

_____

_____

▶ **Pair** Discuss your list. Which actions led to positive resolutions? What is the best advice for someone who has a bad temper or gets angry easily?

In this lesson, you will
- give constructive criticism.
- respond to criticism and give excuses.

Interpersonal Relations

 **Listen and read an article about communication skills.**

Communication is the essence of social interaction. It influences what others think about you and how well they understand you. Look at the following advice for improving your communication skills.

Observe
Communication is a two-way operation that involves sending and receiving signals. Good communicators learn to receive signals so that they can be proactive rather than reactive to what they send. When communicating, step into the shoes of the other person. Read body language, tone of voice, statements, and silences. Investigate the person's motivation and fears.

Ask open-ended questions
Remember, your goal is to get enough information so that you can work with the person to resolve problems. A yes/no (or closed) question will only give you a yes or no answer. A question that begins with "why" puts people on the defensive. Think about how you react when asked questions such as, "Why were you late? Why do you act like that?" Who, what, where, and how questions involve the other person. "What leads you to make that decision? How can we work together on solving this problem? Who else is affected when you're late? When do you think you can start working toward this new goal?"

Frame your responses using the I-messages technique
Essentially you are taking responsibility for your feelings. To begin, comment on observable factual behaviors and state the consequences. Finish with involving the person in a collaborative resolution.

Here's an example: "When you give me your reports at the last minute (fact), I feel frustrated because I must rush and wonder if I'm not catching errors and I end up barking at you (give consequences that matter to them). I wish you would give me more lead time (ask for behavior change in terms of 'start doing *a*' versus 'stop doing *b*') so that we'll both be less stressed (state the benefits). What do you think?"

Match your words to your body language
If you're honest, your body language will confirm it. If you're feeling angry and denying it, your tone of voice might give you away. Be honest, then do a body check to make sure your words match your nonverbal gestures. Otherwise, you won't be taken seriously.

Source: http://www.businesstown.com/people/communication-skills.asp

▶ **Pair** Are you good at communicating with other people? Why is it important to be a good communicator?

1 Getting Along with Your Colleagues

How well do you communicate with your classmates and colleagues? Take a test to find out. Examine the statements and indicate the degree to which they apply to you by putting a check (✔) in the appropriate box.

	Almost Never 1	Rarely 2	Sometimes 3	Quite often 4	Most of the time 5
1. People believe what I'm saying.					
2. I manage to explain my ideas clearly.					
3. When I don't understand a question, I ask for additional explanation.					
4. I find it easy to see things from someone else's point of view.					
5. I find it easy to express my feelings.					
6. I can detect the mood of others when I look at them.					
7. When I'm wrong, I'm not afraid to admit it.					
8. The best way to help others understand me is to tell them what I feel, think, and believe.					
9. I don't become defensive when I'm being criticized.					
10. When I make a criticism, I make sure I refer to the person's actions and behavior, rather than to the person.					

Source: Interpersonal Communications Skills Test,
http://www.queendom.com/tests/communic.html

Count the points for each answer and add up your score. Look at the scoring guide. What kind of communication skills do you have?

      50 – 41 good   40 – 21 average   20 – 10 poor

2 Rick's such a clear speaker.

Mr. Sanchez is preparing performance reports for his staff. He's writing his observations on a legal pad. Complete his observations with *so* or *such a/an*.

> Rick is **such a clear** speaker ⌉
>
>   ⌐— **(that)** people have no problem understanding him
>
> Rick's ideas are **so clear** ⌋

1. Ivan is _____ credible speaker that everybody believes him.

2. Rick is _____ accurate accountant that his books balance every month.

3. Cindy is _____ careful that she always asks for additional information.

4. Ben is _____ energetic assistant that I need to remind him who the boss is.

5. Maria is _____ flexible that she can see things from someone else's point of view.

6. Sara is _____ sensitive person that she finds it easy to express her feelings.

7. Judith is _____ sure of herself that she doesn't become defensive when she's being criticized.

8. Susan is _____ perceptive person that she can detect the mood of others by looking at them.

9. I'm _____ confident that I'm not afraid to admit when I'm wrong.

3 Tell me about what happened.

▶**Pair** Classify the items into situations that encourage or discourage communication between people. Write *E* in front of the items that *encourage* and *D* in front of those that *discourage* communication.

_____ 1. I'd like to sit down with you to help you solve this problem."

_____ 2. "Tell me about what happened."

_____ 3. The listener is silent, but attentive.

_____ 4. "You had better do this or else."

_____ 5. "What made you do something like that?"

_____ 6. "What seems to be the matter?"

_____ 7. "You're wrong. That's stupid."

_____ 8. The listener nods his or her head.

Discuss how you would respond in each of these situations. Write your responses.

1. **A:** Your work hasn't been up to standard lately. What seems to be the matter?
   B: <u>I've been so worried about my mother's health that I can't concentrate on the job.</u>

2. **A:** I heard that you came in late every day last week. Tell me what happened.
   B: _____

3. **A:** Mike told me you've made a number of mistakes in the accounts. I'd like to sit down with you to help you solve this problem.
   B: _____

4 I feel so frustrated.

▶**Pair** A good way to provide constructive criticism is through a method known as I-messages. Using this method, you clearly state what the problem is (without blaming the other person), the way the situation makes you feel, and the effect it has on you. Think of some conflict situations at home, work, or school and write I-messages that could help you.

State problem	Your feeling	Effect on you
"When . . ."	"I get [feel]"	"because"
When you give me your reports at the last minute,	I feel frustrated	because I have to rush and wonder if I'm not catching errors.

▶**Class** Share your I-messages about your conflict situations.

5 Online

Log onto http://www.prenhall.com/brown_activities
The Web: Developing Skills
Grammar: What's your grammar IQ?
E-mail: Five Years from Now

6 Wrap Up

Group List five characteristics of a good coworker (or classmate) and five characteristics of a good supervisor (or teacher).

Coworker (or classmate)	Supervisor (or Teacher)
1. hard-working	1. expert listener
2.	2.
3.	3.
4.	4.
5.	5.

Class Compare your list with those of the other groups.

Strategies for Success

> ➤ Role-playing how to make complaints
> ➤ Planning writing strategies
> ➤ Focusing on differences between English and your native language

1. With a partner, role play the following situations. Make sure you concentrate on the specific grammar and vocabulary you use in the situations. (1) complaining to a waiter about a cold, tasteless meal; (2) returning a defective product to a store; (3) changing to a new hotel room because the one they gave you was not clean.

2. In your journal for this unit, think of goals that you can set for doing more *writing* in English. List those goals specifically (for example, "I will write 10 e-mail messages this week.")

3. With a partner, list some major differences between English and your native language—several very difficult grammar points or pronunciation issues. Make a list of those difficulties and try to concentrate for this week on correcting those parts of your English.

CHECKPOINT

How much have you learned in this unit? Review the goals for each lesson. What skills can you confidently use now? What skills do you need to practice? List these below.

Skills I've Learned Well

_____

_____

_____

_____

Skills I Need to Practice

_____

_____

_____

_____

Learning Preferences

In this unit, which type of activity did you like the best and the least? Write the number in the box: 1 = best; 2 = next best; 3 = next; 4 = least.

❑ Working by myself   ❑ Working with a group

❑ Working with a partner   ❑ Working as a whole class

In this unit, which exercises helped you to learn to:

listen more effectively?   Exercise _____   read more easily?   Exercise _____

speak more fluently?   Exercise _____   write more clearly?   Exercise _____

Which exercise did you like the most? _____   Why? _____

Which exercise did you like the least? _____   Why? _____

Vocabulary

Verbs
argue
balance
detect
get stuck
interfere
regret
rush

Adjectives
competing   rude
credible   stubborn
distracted   virtual
jealous
perceptive

Nouns
bonus
environment
perfectionist
raise
scholarship
stock option

Adverbs
simultaneously

Expressions
calm down
cool off
I'm fed up.
I've had it (with someone or something).
(two weeks) in advance
lose one's temper
see (something) through
take it easy
work out (a problem)

The passive voice in the future

The food **will be catered.**

The passive voice with modals

He	may		sent	on more business trips.
Traveling	might	be	done	in a virtual world created by computers.
Schools	could		abolished	because students will be taught via the Internet.
Customers	should		given	quality service.

Modals in the past (perfect modals)

Tyler	should			suggested	all those bells and whistles.
I	could			done	something wrong.
The meeting	may/must	[not]	have	lasted	longer than she expected.
She	might			heard.	

Hope

Nelson hopes (that) he can make some improvements.
Nelson hopes to make some improvements.

Result clauses with *so . . . (that)*

Rick's ideas are **so** clear **(that)** people have no problem understanding him.

Result clauses with *such, a/an . . . (that)*

Rick is **such a** clear speaker **(that)** people have no problem understanding him.

Talking about changes
Customers will be given high-quality service.

Stating rules
No children are allowed at work.

Expressing hope
Nelson hopes to make some improvements.

Speculating about the future
Traveling will be done in a virtual world created by computers.

Drawing conclusions
She might not have heard.

Expressing anger
I'm fed up with this project.

Responding to anger
It's OK. Calm down.

Persuading someone not to act impulsively
It'll work out. Try to see it through.

Talking about past advisability
I should have told you about my problems.

Talking about possibilities
If Anna hasn't come yet, the meeting may have lasted longer than expected.

Giving constructive criticism
Your work hasn't been up to standard lately. What seems to be the matter?

Responding to criticism and giving excuses
I've been so worried about my mother's health that I can't concentrate on the job.

UNIT 9

Lesson 1

In this lesson, you will

- speculate about future events.
- talk about hypothetical situations.
- make assumptions about the past.

Friendship in the Workplace

🔊 **Lynn and her coworker Eva, a social worker from Venezuela, are leaving work to go home. The two are friendly with each other but aren't close friends. Eva notices that Lynn seems upset about something and decides to ask her about it. Listen to their conversation.**

Eva: Lynn, you seem worried about something. Is everything OK?

Lynn: Everything's fine.

Eva: Are you sure? You look upset.

Lynn: It's no big deal.

Eva: Well, you can always talk to me if you want. You might feel better if you do.

Lynn: Thanks, but I don't like to discuss my feelings at work.

Eva: Then it must have been very disappointing that I told Ms. Price how you felt about your promotion.

Lynn: Oh, Eva, you mustn't think that I'm upset with you! I'm just annoyed at myself for not being able to accept Ms. Price's praise of my work in front of the whole office.

Eva: Why was that difficult for you?

Lynn: Well, being singled out makes me feel awkward and embarrassed.

Eva: That's hard for me to understand, but I'm glad you explained it to me. As you know, I'm rather outspoken.

Lynn: Yes, I saw you the other day letting production know what you thought about their procedures.

Eva: And believe me, it worked. They're going to make a few adjustments to solve the delay problems we've been having lately.

Lynn: That'll be great for all of us.

Eva: I certainly hope so. By the way, I'm having a picnic at the park on Saturday. Would you like to come?

Lynn: I'd love to. Can I bring anything?

Eva: Just yourself!

Lynn: You know, I'm feeling better already.

▶ **Pair** If someone is angry or upset, do you think it's better for that person to talk about how he or she feels? Or is it better to keep feelings inside? Explain your answer.

1 Are you an open book?

Some people are like open books. They're so up front with their feelings that it's easy to know them well. Others are mysterious and full of surprises. Even their closest friends can't guess how they really feel. Take the Open Book Test to find out how open you are. Examine the statements and indicate the degree to which they apply to you by putting a check (✔) in the appropriate box.

Open Book Test

	Very inaccurate 1	Somewhat inaccurate 2	Somewhat accurate 3	Very accurate 4
1. What I'm feeling is written all over my face.	○	○	○	○
2. I'm like a stage actor who never wears a mask.	○	○	○	○
3. My friends all know my life story.	○	○	○	○
4. I never try to keep others from knowing the real me.	○	○	○	○
5. My close friends know just about everything about me.	○	○	○	○
6. It's easy for me to open up to others and share my feelings.	○	○	○	○
7. The person I am is the person others see.	○	○	○	○
8. I never keep my personal feelings to myself.	○	○	○	○
9. I like to tell personal stories to my friends.	○	○	○	○
10. My friends always know what will make me happy or sad.	○	○	○	○

Based on: http://www.emode.com/emode/tests/open_book.jsp

▶**Pair** Add up your points and read the article in Exercise 2 for your detailed test results. Then discuss the results with your partner.

2 You're easy to read.

If you scored between 31 and 40, cover to cover, you are definitely a wide open book. If you feel a certain mood, you express it immediately. Because there's so little to hide within your emotional pages, you're easy to read. Your closest friends know you quite well, and can read your face like a book.

If you scored between 21 and 30, you don't want to hide behind a thick cover. Most of the time you prefer to express yourself and get things off your chest. That's not to say that everything is open material. Your answers indicate that some chapters are off limits. Maybe you'll open up to some close acquaintances—but other feelings stay wrapped up tight among your emotional private papers.

If you scored between 11 and 20, your score shows how much you value your privacy. Your emotions are not out there in broad circulation—you prefer to keep them hidden on the shelf. Clearly, there are many "chapters" of your life kept off limits, even from close friends.

If you scored 10, your tough exterior makes it especially hard to get a good read on your emotions. Instead of expressing how you feel, you prefer to keep things tucked away. It's difficult for you to get things out in the open. You prefer to hold them in.

▶Pair List the underlined expressions on page 112 under the appropriate category.

Talking about feelings	Keeping feelings to oneself
easy to read	hidden on the shelf

3 You can read their faces like a book.

Listen to the cassette. Then read each statement and mark it *T* (true) or *F* (false).

_____ 1. People in different countries experience different emotions.

_____ 2. Children learn how to express their emotions by watching their parents.

_____ 3. It's always easy to know what another person is thinking.

_____ 4. If you seem upset about something, an American will often ask, "What's wrong?"

_____ 5. Americans think not talking about emotions is a sign of maturity.

_____ 6. Boys and girls are taught to express sadness in the same way.

4 If Lynn rides on the carousel, she might get dizzy.

▶Pair Lynn is in the park with Eva, Eva's husband Carlos, and their two children, Marcos and Luisa. Look at each picture and talk about what *will*, *might*, or *could* happen.

1. Lynn/ride on the carousel

2. Marcos and Luisa/play on the swings

3. Luisa/go down the slide

4. Marcos and Luisa/ride their bikes in the park

5. Marcos and Carlos/go on the seesaw

6. Luisa/play in the sand

5 What would you do if . . . ?

►**Mixer** Answer the questions for yourself. Then ask a classmate what he or she would do if these situations occurred in the park.

What would you do if . . .	I would	Classmate's name
1. a dog got off its leash and started to growl at you?		
2. it started to thunder and lightning when you were in the swimming pool?		
3. you and your friends brought a huge picnic, and there were no more picnic tables available?		
4. a child fell and cut his knee and you couldn't find his parents?		
5. you were riding your bike and you got a flat tire?		

6 They must have been enjoying themselves.

►**Pair** Look at the pictures and make assumptions about what the people *must/may have been* doing.

1. Eva and Carlos spent all evening at the club.

They must have been dancing.

2. They took off their boots and soaked their feet in warm water.

_____

3. I saw Ivan and Gina buying $100 worth of snack foods.

_____

4. Jim and Tina won first prize.

_____

5. Debbie's feet were really freezing.

_____

6. Jean had a bad sunburn when she got home.

_____

Lesson 2

In this lesson, you will
- talk about past possibility.
- talk about past advisability.
- talk about wishes.

Going Home for a Visit

🎧 **Listen and read.**

Gina: Are you crying?

Lynn: No. Just choked up. I think my mother's sick.

Gina: How do you know your mother's ill? You talked to her this morning, didn't you?

Lynn: Yes, I did, but she didn't sound so good. I think she's very sick.

Gina: She could have been tired.

Lynn: How about last week? I called several times, but she wasn't home. She may have been in the hospital.

Gina: You don't know that.

Lynn: I should have gone back in the summer when she asked me to. I even booked a ticket, but then I changed my mind.

Gina: But you were busy with getting ready for college and your new job.

Lynn: Still, I could have gone before I started the job.

Gina: Stop that, Lynn.

Lynn: I wish I could take a week off and go, but I may lose my job if I do.

Gina: You can go back for Christmas. It's only three months away.

Lynn: Do you know what bothers me? I can't stop thinking that she might have been sick last summer, and that's why she wanted me to go back.

Gina: You just feel guilty because you said no to your mom.

Lynn: She sounded disappointed when I told her I was too busy to go back.

Gina: She might have been, but I'm sure she understands.

Lynn: I hope so . . . Anyway, thanks for being such a good friend. Maybe we can go to China together for Christmas.

Gina: I wish I could go, but my family and I are planning to spend the holidays together in Italy.

Lynn: Well, I guess we should have gone together last summer.

Gina: Stop all this *should have, could have.* Let's get something to eat and go see a movie. Call your sister and ask her if your mom's ill.

▶**Pair** **Have you made any choices in the past that you regret? Tell your partner what happened.**

1 Lynn could have taken a week off from work to visit her family.

▶**Pair** Lynn is having a bad dream. In her dream, her mother is seriously ill, and different people are telling her what she *could have* done. What advice did each of them give her?

1. Lynn: I was too busy at work.

   Father: _____

2. Lynn: I didn't have enough money for the plane ticket.

   Aunt: _____

3. Lynn: I was afraid they'd ask me to stay and not go back to the United States.

   Sister: _____

4. Lynn: I was worried I'd lose my job.

   Brother: _____

2 Lynn's mother may have been tired.

▶**Pair** Lynn had assumed her mother was ill based on the following clues. Suggest some possible explanations of what *may have, might have,* or *could have* been the cause.

1. Her mother sounded out of breath when Lynn talked to her on the phone.

   _____

2. Her mother wasn't home even when Lynn called late at night.

   _____

3. Her sister postponed her business trip.

   _____

4. Her father asked her when she could come to visit them.

   _____

5. She got a call in the middle of the night, but when she picked up the phone, there was no one on the other end.

   _____

3 Lynn should have been more careful.

▶ **Pair** Because Lynn has been worrying about her mother, she's made some careless mistakes in the past week. Look at each picture and decide what she *shouldn't have* done and what she *should have* done instead.

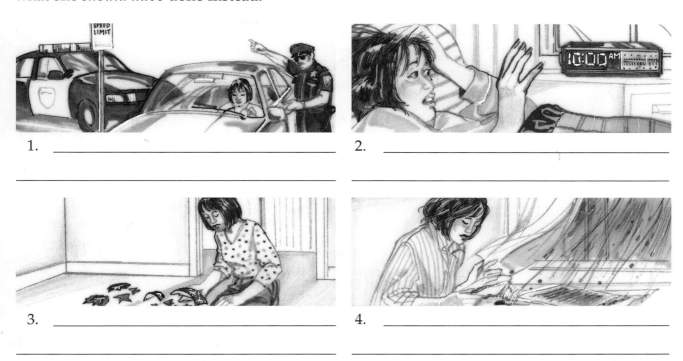

1. _____

_____

2. _____

3. _____

_____

4. _____

_____

4 If Lynn had gone home last summer, her mother would have been delighted.

Complete the sentences following the examples in the box.

> If Lynn **had gone** home last summer, her mother **would have been** delighted.
>
> Lynn's mother **would have been** delighted if she **had gone** home last summer.

1. If she had seen her mother last summer, Lynn _____
   _____.

2. Lynn would have gone home last summer if she _____
   _____.

3. If Lynn hadn't been getting ready for college, _____
   _____.

4. Gina would have agreed to go to China in December if she _____
   _____.

5. Lynn would have seen for herself how her mother was if _____
   _____.

5 What do you wish?

Mixer Sometimes people wish things were different. What do your classmates wish? Interview three classmates and write their answers to the questions in the chart.

> What do you wish you owned?
> I wish I owned a new car.

	Name	Name	Name
1. Where do you wish you lived?			
2. What do you wish you were (occupation)?			
3. What do you wish you could buy?			
4. Where do you wish you could go on vacation?			
5. What do you wish you didn't have to do?			

Class Report your classmates' wishes to the class.

6 Nelson wishes his team got along better.

Pair Read about the situations people are encountering at their jobs. State what they *wish* would or could be different.

> I wish our work environment were more pleasant.
> I wish my coworkers could get along better.

1. Sofia got an *F* on her final paper. She got an *F* for the course.

   _____

2. Lynn was upset because Gina invited some friends over on Saturday night without asking her first.

   _____

3. Ivan accidentally deleted some files on a coworker's computer while he was trying to fix it. He feels that it was a careless error.

   _____

4. Lynn is unhappy because Gina can't go home to China with her this year.

   _____

7 He could have been cordial.

Group Look at these tips for resolving conflicts at work. Imagine yourself in the situations and decide how you *would have, could have,* or *should have* handled each one. Use the tips from the Dos and Don'ts or your own ideas.

1. A colleague who has been with the company for a long time feels superior to you because of intimate, first-hand knowledge of the business. This person has just told you that the report you wrote does not accurately reflect the position of the company.

2. One of your employees spends a great deal of time complaining about long hours and not being appreciated. This person has just told you that you didn't give him/her enough lead time to finish the report you need for a client.

3. The boss's secretary aggressively guards the boss's office, screens every caller, and uses limited power to its full extent. This person has just told you that the report you submitted for the boss's approval has been mysteriously misplaced.

Dos
• Be cordial and nonthreatening in manner, tone, and speech.
• Give words of sympathy the employee feels are deserved but are seldom received.
• Acknowledge the advice with a quiet "I see," and then move on to another task.
• Avoid the employee as much as possible.
• Ask appropriate questions to indicate that you respect the person's position and ideas.

Don'ts
• Ignore the employee or try to bypass the person's authority.
• Give the person the opportunity of pointing out your mistakes.
• Suggest new ways of doing things.
• Offer help or make a suggestion.
• Get tricked into handling the person's work.

Lesson 3

In this lesson, you will
- talk about present conditions.

Talking over Problems

Sofia and a classmate are looking at a poster of a conflict-resolution workshop. Listen to their conversation.

Sofia: Irene, look at this flyer . . . a workshop on conflict resolution. Hmm, do you ever go to things like this?

Irene: Sure. They're great. They probably save lots of relationships.

Sofia: Do people actually feel comfortable talking about these things outside of their families?

Irene: You don't have to talk about the details. These workshops just give you tools for solving problems. If you want to talk about something specific, you make an appointment to see a counselor.

Sofia: A total stranger? I couldn't do that.

Irene: So what do you do when you have a problem?

Sofia: I tell a friend or someone in my family.

Irene: That's interesting. Come to think of it, I tend to trust professional therapists more than my family.

Sofia: I'm amazed to hear you say that.

Irene: It's not such a big deal if you see a counselor. I mean it's not embarrassing. No one thinks there's anything wrong with you.

Sofia: I'm not against it . . . really, but I'm not sure I'd be comfortable doing it. I was thinking about my cousin Jamileh and her parents. They're arguing a lot. Her parents want her to go to medical school, and she doesn't want to go. If she or her parents went to something like this, maybe they could get help to work out their differences. I bet they'd never do it though.

Irene: Why don't you go? Then maybe you can help them.

Sofia: Yeah, maybe I'll do that.

Pair Who do you talk to when you have a problem? Why do you choose that person?

1 I'm willing to give up a lot to end this conflict.

🔊 **Listen to the speaker talk about different styles for dealing with conflicts. Then match each term with its meaning.**

____	1.	avoidance	a. I'm willing to give up a lot to end this conflict.
____	2.	accommodation	b. If we discuss this, we can find a solution that everyone likes.
____	3.	aggression	c. It's not a big problem. Why rock the boat?
____	4.	compromise	d. There are winners and losers. I want to be the winner.
____	5.	problem solving	e. I'll give a little if you give a little.

▶**Group** **Which form of conflict resolution do you usually use? Why?**

2 I don't argue with my parents unless it's very important.

Complete each sentence.

Example:

I don't give in **unless** I'm convinced that I'm wrong.

1. We can't resolve our differences unless
   _____
   _____

2. I understand how you feel. You don't have to have surgery unless _____
   _____

3. I don't join in their arguments unless
   _____
   _____

4. I will not compromise unless _____
   _____
   _____

▶**Group** **What is each person's style of conflict resolution?**

3 Online

Log onto http://www.prenhall.com/brown_activities
The Web: Personality
Grammar: What's your grammar IQ?
E-mail: If I Won the Lottery

4 Wrap Up

▶**Pair** On a small sheet of paper, write a brief description of a conflict situation at work or at home that you need help with. Put your slip of paper in a small box at the front of the room with the slips of the other members of the class.

▶**Class** Take turns taking one slip of paper out of the box and offering some advice. Ask other students to add to your advice.

▶**Pair** Listen to the advice given for your problem and select the one you think is the best for you. Write a paragraph stating which advice you choose to follow and why.

Strategies for Success

➤ **Using expressions that describe personalities**
➤ **Practicing reading strategies**
➤ **Making your mistakes work *for* you**

1. With a partner, look back at Exercises 1, 2, and 3 in Lesson 1, where you thought about *yourself* as either an "open book" or not. Use as many of the expressions in Exercise 2 to describe two or three *other* people you each know, and give examples to support your description.

2. In your journal for this unit, think of goals that you can set for doing more *reading* in English. List those goals specifically (for example, "I will read 20 pages of English this week.")

3. With a partner, tell each other stories about places you *wish* you had traveled to and why. When you listen to your partner, write down *any* grammar mistakes your partner makes. Show your partner the list. Over the next week or more, try to notice when *you* make any of those grammar mistakes, and see if you can say the sentences correctly after a week.

CHECKPOINT

How much have you learned in this unit? Review the goals for each lesson. What skills can you confidently use now? What skills do you need to practice? List these below.

Skills I've Learned Well

_____
_____
_____
_____

Skills I Need to Practice

_____
_____
_____
_____

Learning Preferences

In this unit, which type of activity did you like the best and the least? Write the number in the box: 1 = best; 2 = next best; 3 = next; 4 = least.

❏ Working by myself   ❏ Working with a group
❏ Working with a partner   ❏ Working as a whole class

In this unit, which exercises helped you to learn to:

listen more effectively?   Exercise _____   read more easily?   Exercise _____

speak more fluently?   Exercise _____   write more clearly? Exercise _____

Which exercise did you like the most? _____   Why? _____

Which exercise did you like the least? _____   Why? _____

Vocabulary

Nouns	Verbs	Expressions
adjustment	compromise	easy to read
carousel	lightning	get things off your chest
conflict resolution	open (up)	get things out in the open
delay	postpone	hold (something) in
mask	soak	off limits
sand	thunder	read (someone) like a book
seesaw	**Adjectives**	
slide	awkward	
swing		

► GRAMMAR SUMMARY

Review: The conditional in real or possible situations

If Lynn gets on the carousel, she	will enjoy it. might get dizzy.

Review: The conditional in hypothetical situations

What **would** you do if you were riding your bike and got a flat tire?

The conditional in unreal situations in the past

If Lynn **had gone** home last summer,	her mother **would have been** delighted.
Lynn's mother **would have been** delighted	if she **had gone** home last summer.

Modals in the progressive

Present	They	**must**	**be**	**eating** lunch.
Past	They	**must**	**have been**	**dancing.**

Modals in the past (perfect modals)

I	**could**			**gone**	before I started the job.
	should	(not)	have	**gone**	back in the summer.
She	**might/may**			**been**	tired.

Wish

Hypothetical Situations	I wish I owned a new car.
Wishes	I wish my coworkers would get along better.

Unless

I	**don't**	**give** in	**unless**	I'm convinced that I'm wrong.

► COMMUNICATION SUMMARY

Speculating about future events

If Lynn gets on the carousel, she might get dizzy.

Talking about hypothetical situations

What would you do if you were riding your bike and got a flat tire?

Making assumptions about the past

They must have been dancing.

Talking about past possibility

Lynn's mother may/might have been tired.
If Lynn had gone home last summer, her mother would have been delighted.

Talking about past advisability

Lynn should have been more careful.

Talking about wishes

I wish my coworkers would get along better.

Talking about present conditions

I don't argue with my parents unless it's very important.

Lesson 1

In this lesson, you will
- talk about having/getting something done.
- report opinions, thoughts, and feelings.

Getting Together

🔊 **Ivan, Nelson, and Tony are getting together with Lynn and Gina in their apartment. They're reminiscing about old times. Listen and read.**

Gina: Do you realize that we've known each other for three years?

Nelson: Has it been that long?

Lynn: I remember when I first met Yumiko . . . at the airport.

Tony: And I remember when I ran into you too . . . I had just had my courses approved and was on my way to the cafeteria.

Nelson: And how could we ever forget meeting Pablo on the beach in Mexico!

Ivan: The Piñata Caper!

Gina: Well, I certainly miss Mrs. Brennan. I wonder how she's doing.

Lynn: Oh, I forgot to tell you that Yumiko saw Mrs. Brennan in Tokyo.

Gina: In Tokyo? What was she doing in Tokyo?

Lynn: Mr. Brennan was on assignment there, and they looked Yumiko up to say hello. They'll be in Spain next month, Yumiko said.

Tony: Spain? I bet they'll visit Oscar.

Ivan: Hey, I have a thought. Pablo said he'd be spending his vacation with Oscar next month. How about a reunion in Spain?

Gina: That's a wonderful idea! My parents are spending two weeks in Milan, and I can stop off in Spain before I meet them there.

Nelson: Well, that leaves me out. We're upgrading our entire network system this summer, and I really can't get away.

Lynn: Me too. I'd love to go. But I have to go home to China to see my mother.

Tony: Well, I'm available. Count me in!

▶ **Pair** **Have you ever had a class or family reunion? How did you feel seeing people you hadn't seen for a long time? What did you talk about?**

1 Gina had her passport renewed.

▶Pair Gina is getting ready for the reunion in Spain. Look at the pictures and discuss the things she *had done* or *got done*.

| She **had** her passport **renewed**. | She **got** her camera **repaired**. |

1. renew passport

2. change money

3. fix camera

4. dry-clean clothes

5. cut hair

6. manicure nails

7. stop newspaper

8. turn off electricity

2 I'd like to have this film developed.

Listen to the conversation and practice it with a partner. Then make up a similar conversation about one of the items in the checklist.

A: Can I help you?

B: Yes, I'd like to have this camera repaired.

A: Will there be anything else?

B: Well, while I'm here, I might as well get this film developed.

To Do List

✔ cut hair
✔ press pants
✔ repair watch
✔ fix brakes
✔ shine shoes

✔ shampoo hair
✔ clean blouses
✔ change watch battery
✔ wash car
✔ replace heels

▶Group Perform your conversation for the group. Then tell your group about some things you need to have done.

3 Could you get someone to photocopy these papers?

▶**Pair** Lynn is going downtown. She asks Gina if she can do anything for her while she's out. Complete their conversation, using *have* something done or *get* someone to do what is needed.

	Active Construction			Passive Construction	
I'll	**have** **fix**	someone	the camera.	I'll	**have** the camera **fixed**.
	get **to fix**			**get**	

Lynn: I'm going downtown. Is there anything you need?

Gina: Well, if you go by a drugstore, I'd like to _____.
(1. fill this prescription)

Lynn: I've got to go to Premier Drugs anyway. They have a photocopier and I need to _____. I can drop your prescription off then.
(2. copy some papers)

Gina: Oh, and my camera is broken. I have to _____. Will you be
(3. look at it)
going by a camera shop?

Lynn: I need to go to the dry cleaner's. The dress I wore yesterday has a big coffee stain, and I really need to _____. There's a good camera shop next door.
(4. clean it)

Gina: Say, while you're there . . . the hem on this skirt is falling down. They always do alterations for me. Could you _____?
(5. fix it)

Lynn: Sure, no problem.

4 He was truly an amazing artist.

🔊 Gina, Tony, Oscar, and Ivan are talking about their plans and their impressions of Spain. Listen to their conversation. Then read the sentences below and mark each one *T* (True) or *F* (False).

  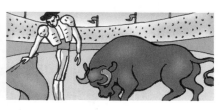

_____ 1.   Gina doesn't think that flamenco is an exciting musical experience.

_____ 2.   Ivan believes that Russian music is preferable to Spanish music.

_____ 3.   Tony thinks that a bullfight will be an exciting experience.

_____ 4.   Gina agrees that bullfighting is something exciting to see.

_____ 5.   Ivan says that eating is one of the best Spanish popular customs.

_____ 6.   Gina believes that Spanish food is good for her diet.

_____ 7.   Ivan understands that Paella Valenciana is a delicious Spanish dessert.

_____ 8.   Gina feels that going to the Prado Museum to see the great Spanish artists is the best way to spend the day.

Pair Listen to the conversation on page 127 again and select one of the topics discussed in it. Look up the topic on the Internet or in an encyclopedia. Tell your partner what you have learned. Then your partner reports what you've said to the class. Use *feel, say, believe, agree, think* + *that* in your statements.

5 I think that it's too late for Pablo to go to the bank.

Pair It's Monday afternoon at 2:00, and Gina, Oscar, Pablo, and Tony have spent the whole morning at Retiro Park. Read "Hours in Madrid" from *Tourist Tips* to see if they will be able to do the things listed below. Why or why not?

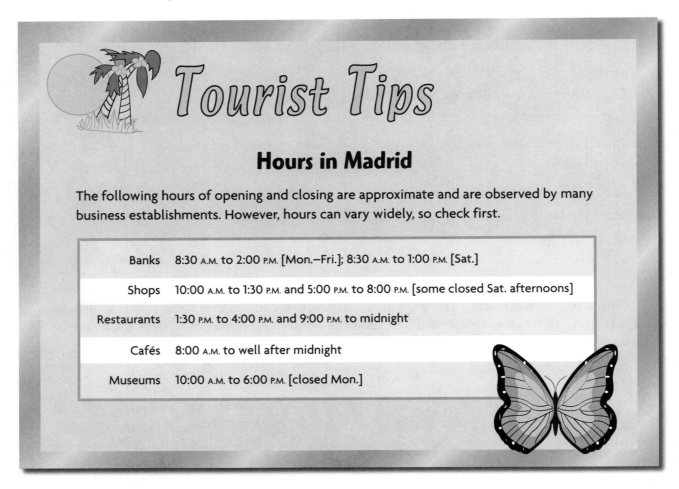

Tourist Tips

Hours in Madrid

The following hours of opening and closing are approximate and are observed by many business establishments. However, hours can vary widely, so check first.

Banks	8:30 A.M. to 2:00 P.M. [Mon.–Fri.]; 8:30 A.M. to 1:00 P.M. [Sat.]
Shops	10:00 A.M. to 1:30 P.M. and 5:00 P.M. to 8:00 P.M. [some closed Sat. afternoons]
Restaurants	1:30 P.M. to 4:00 P.M. and 9:00 P.M. to midnight
Cafés	8:00 A.M. to well after midnight
Museums	10:00 A.M. to 6:00 P.M. [closed Mon.]

1. Pablo wants to change some money at the bank.
2. Gina wants to go to some small shops to look for gifts.
3. Tony wants to have lunch.
4. Oscar wants to go to the Prado museum.

Class Imagine that you're going to take a vacation in Spain. Look for information on the Internet or do some library research. Decide where you want to go and write two or three short paragraphs explaining why. Mention things such as weather, food, daytime and nighttime activities, language, or anything else that makes this place attractive to you. Then read your paragraphs to the class.

Lesson 2

In this lesson, you will

- report what other people asked or said.
- express advice.
- report other people's opinions.

Dating in the Workplace

Lynn's coworkers are talking about her. Listen and read.

Mrs. Chin: Did you give Lynn a ride home yesterday?

Lee: Who told you that I did?

Mrs. Chin: Celia. She said you give her a ride quite often. I guess people have noticed that you're spending a lot of time with Lynn.

Lee: Oh, really? What else are people saying?

Mrs. Chin: Oh, well, people around here love to talk about everyone in the office . . . but, uh, are you interested in Lynn?

Lee: Lynn's a great person, and right now she's homesick.

Mrs. Chin: Uh-huh . . . , go on.

Lee: What? Did someone tell you that I spent too much time in Lynn's office?

Mrs. Chin: No, of course not, but Mr. Nichols asked me if you two were dating. I told him I'd try to find out.

Lee: Oh, man! Thank you for telling me.

Mrs. Chin: You're welcome, but is there anything going on between you two? I think it can be very awkward for two people who are dating to work together.

Lee: Mrs. Chin, Lynn and I are both professionals.

Mrs. Chin: Don't be so defensive, Lee. Anyone can see that you like each other.

Lee: I didn't know it was so obvious. Lynn's a very private person. She'd be very uncomfortable if she knew that people were gossiping about us.

Mrs. Chin: I understand. I just want to tell Mr. Nichols that there's nothing to worry about.

Lee: OK, please tell him we can handle it, and please don't tell Lynn about our conversation.

▶ **Pair** What do you think about employees dating each other?

1 She said that people were talking about us.

▶**Pair** Lynn is telling Gina what she overheard in the cafeteria. Use the model below to change the statements she heard (page 129) to reported speech.

Mrs. Chin: People have noticed that you're spending a lot of time with Lynn.	**Lynn:** Mrs. Chin said (that) people had noticed that Lee was spending a lot of time with me.
Lee: Well, she lives near me.	**Lynn:** Lee said (that) I lived near him.

Gina: What's the matter? Did something happen to you at work? You sound really upset.

Lynn: Yes, something happened today that I'm really embarassed about.

Gina: Oh, my goodness, tell me everything.

Lynn: I overheard Mrs. Chin talking to my friend Lee in the cafeteria. She said (1)_____
_____.

Gina: Did that bother you?

Lynn: No, not at first, but then Mrs. Chin mentioned that our boss, Mr. Nichols, had asked her if we were dating. She said (2)_____.

Gina: Oh, so do you think Lee likes you?

Lynn: Yes, maybe. He was very sweet. He was worried about my privacy. He said (3)_____
_____.

Mrs. Chin said she understood. She said (4)_____
_____.

What do you think?

Gina: Well, do you like Lee?

Lynn: I don't know him well enough to be sure, but he is polite and funny. (*sigh*) Yes, I do like him.

2 Gina asked Lynn if something had happened to her.

▶**Pair** Report to your partner on the questions that Gina asked Lynn.

Did something happen to you at work?	Gina asked Lynn if something had happened to her.
Did that bother you?	
Do you think Lee likes you?	
Do you like Lee?	

▶**Class** Do you think Lynn should go out with Lee? Discuss and then report your opinions to the class.

3 Mrs. Chin asked Lynn if she liked the company.

Mrs. Chin has made an appointment to talk to Lynn over lunch. Read the questions. Check (✔) the questions that would be appropriate for Mrs. Chin to ask.

_____ 1. Are you and Lee going out on the weekends?

_____ 2. Does your supervisor know that you and Lee are spending time together?

_____ 3. Do your parents know about you and Lee?

_____ 4. Is your relationship interfering with your work?

_____ 5. Are you aware of company policy on employees' dating?

_____ 6. Did you discuss the situation at work with Lee?

Pair Now listen to the tape. Which questions did Mrs. Chin actually ask? What do you think of Mrs. Chin's questions?

Listen to the tape again. What advice did Mrs. Chin give Lynn? What do you think of her advice? Share your opinions with the class.

4 What would you tell her?

Look at the pictures. Write what you would tell each person to do and not to do.

I would **tell her to be** supportive.	I would **tell her not to** interfere.

I just want to help.

I don't know what to do.

I like Lynn, and I want to continue spending time with her.

5 I didn't know she said that.

Lynn and Lee are comparing notes on what people have said about their friendship.
Complete their statements, telling what people said.

Lee	Lynn
1. Mrs Chin: You should take it slowly.	4. Mrs. Chin: Mr. Nichols knows about your friendship with Lee.
2. Mr. Nichols: Don't let your friendship interefere with your work.	5. Gina: These things happen all the time in the workplace.
3. Mrs. Chin's secretary: Lynn is worried about people talking in the office.	6. Mrs. Chin's secretary: You know Lee would never want to cause problems for you.

Lee:

1. Mrs. Chin told me __that we should take it slowly._____

2. Mr. Nichols told me _____.

3. Mrs. Chin's secretary said _____.

Lynn:

4. Mrs. Chin said _____.

5. Gina said _____.

6. Mrs. Chin's secretary told me _____.

6 My partner says he would never date someone at work.

▶ **Pair** Interview your partner. Then share your partner's opinions with the class.

1. How do you feel about coworkers dating?

2. What advice would you give a friend who was dating a coworker?

3. What would you do if you were a supervisor and your employees were dating?

4. What would you do if you were a supervisor and a relationship between your employees ended badly?

5. Would you date a coworker? Under what circumstances?

▶ **Group** Imagine that you are in charge of company policy. Make up a list of rules for relationships between coworkers. Then share your rules with the class.

Lesson 3

In this lesson, you will
- agree and disagree.
- compliment.

Workplace Etiquette

🔊 **Listen and read the advice of Dr. Iris Moody, author of *Workplace Etiquette*.**

OK. So you have survived filling out job applications, doing the interviews, and waiting for the phone calls. The company you have dreamed about has offered you a job, and you have accepted it. All your worries are over now. Or are they?

New research shows that the most stressful part of a job search may be the first few days or weeks on the job. As a new employee, you are walking into an unfamiliar environment. At the same time, you want to make a good impression and build healthy relationships. After all, you may be "living" with these people five days a week for a long time. The following five pointers can help you with the hurdles of office etiquette as you ease into your new job:

Listen: Probably the single most important factor in creating a good relationship is listening. Make eye contact with the person speaking to you and give your full attention. Your colleagues will be willing to share information with you if you show you are willing to hear it.

Respond: When someone speaks, respond by addressing the issue he or she has brought up. Changing the subject abruptly or babbling can be offensive. You may add your own ideas, but do this after acknowledging the other person's point of view.

Do your homework: You may be eager to show your talents and skills in the first few days at your new job, but first you need to understand the dynamics of the office. For example, you need to find out about the process by which decisions are made. Are they made through collaboration, or do they come from the top? In any case, collaborate with your coworkers.

Advance new ideas cautiously: Perhaps you are fresh out of college and full of new ideas, and you can't wait to share them with your colleagues. Although you may be sincere, your coworkers may think that you are criticizing their ways of doing things. This will very likely result in an unfriendly atmosphere. To avoid this unpleasant outcome, first acknowledge the positive aspects of the old methods before you make suggestions for improvement.

Find ways to build relationships: Bring a box of donuts or, if you work in a health-conscious environment, a more nutritious snack, like muffins or fruit, to the office. This will indicate your willingness to befriend others. Although you may be tempted to work through your breaks at first, it may result in your being isolated. Remember that chatting about the job with new colleagues is as important as getting your work done at your desk.

▶ **Pair** **Share with your partner ways of starting a relationship with new classmates or colleagues.**

1 I think that's a good idea.

▶**Pair** Based on the article, choose the most appropriate responses in the following contexts. Explain your choices.

1. You are attending a meeting. The committee leader is explaining a boring idea. You
    a. nod politely and listen.
    b. interrupt and ask what the point is.
    c. take out your notebook and start jotting ideas for another project.
    d. begin a conversation with the person next to you.

2. Your colleagues ask you if you want to go out to lunch with them. You have a lot of work to do. You
    a. thank them and tell them you have too much work to do.
    b. say *sure* and leave your work behind.
    c. suggest that you all have lunch together in the cafeteria.
    d. politely tell them you don't eat lunch.

3. Your new boss is explaining a procedure currently in place. You
    a. tell your boss you know a better way to do it.
    b. listen to your boss and don't mention your idea.
    c. wait to check with a colleague before suggesting your improvement.
    d. summarize your boss's explanation and pose your suggestion in the form of a question.

4. One of your colleagues is telling you about a work-related problem. You
    a. immediately suggest a solution to the problem.
    b. tell your colleague you are too busy to listen to his or her problem.
    c. listen to the problem and ask questions to help clarify the problem for your colleague.
    d. start talking about your own problems.

5. You are working on a team project, and you feel that your ideas are being ignored because you are new at this company. You
    a. hide your feelings from your colleagues.
    b. tell your team members how you feel.
    c. try to prove to your colleagues that you are worth listening to.
    d. tell your boss about your ideas.

▶**Group** Think of some other situations that you have confronted at work or in class. Discuss what happened and what you did to resolve the problem or dilemma.

2 I can't say I agree with you.

 Iris Moody is on a radio talk show, discussing her work with talk-show host Garth Night. Listen to the conversation and fill in the chart based on Garth Night's reaction to the strategies.

Strategies	Agree	Disagree	Reason
Listening Responding Doing your homework Taking time for small talk Advancing new ideas cautiously			

▶**Group** Do you agree with these strategies? Explain why or why not.

3 Online

Log onto http://www.prenhall.com/brown_activities
The Web: Seeing the World
Grammar: What's your grammar IQ?
E-mail: Here's what they said.

4 Wrap Up

▶**Group** You are a member of a committee responsible for making policies regarding workplace etiquette for a company. Devise policies for the following categories. Present your policies to the class and give reasons for each one.

1.   Chatting at work
2.   Dating a coworker
3.   Eating at one's desk
4.   Becoming friends with or dating clients
5.   Using the office equipment for personal reasons
6.   Others _____

Strategies for Success

➤ **Reading aloud with personalized changes**
➤ **Reviewing grammar and setting goals for the future**
➤ **Reviewing your goals from the beginning of the course**

1. With a partner, look at the communication skills you have practiced in this course (listed at the end of each unit). Focus on the last five units, and as you refer to each summary page, look at the example sentences, then *change* each sentence to personalize it to you, your partner, or some of your classmates. For example, on page 137, where "Gina believes that Spanish food is good for her diet," you could read, "I think our teacher was remarkable for her great methods."

2. Continuing with your partner, look at all the grammar points (at the end of each unit) in this book. Help each other to make a list of the points that are still difficult. Each of you should then put your lists in your journal and plan to concentrate on those after this course.

3. Look back again at the goals you set for yourself in Unit 1 (Strategies exercise #3). Did you reach them? If so, in your journal write some more goals to attain after you finish this course. If not, restate them in your journal and plan to accomplish them soon.

CHECKPOINT

How much have you learned in this unit? Review the goals for each lesson. What skills can you confidently use now? What skills do you need to practice? List these below.

Skills I've Learned Well

_____

_____

_____

_____

Skills I Need to Practice

_____

_____

_____

_____

Learning Preferences

In this unit, which type of activity did you like the best and the least? Write the number in the box: 1 = best; 2 = next best; 3 = next; 4 = least.

☐ Working by myself

☐ Working with a partner

☐ Working with a group

☐ Working as a whole class

In this unit, which exercises helped you to learn to:

listen more effectively?   Exercise _____

speak more fluently?   Exercise _____

read more easily?   Exercise _____

write more clearly?   Exercise _____

Which exercise did you like the most? _____   Why? _____

Which exercise did you like the least? _____   Why? _____

Vocabulary

Verbs
advance
dry-clean
manicure
press
renew
repair
replace
shine

Nouns
alteration
heel
hem
stain

Adjectives
supportive

GRAMMAR SUMMARY

Review: active causative

I'll	have	someone	fix	the camera.
	get		to fix	

Passive causative

I'll	have	the camera	fixed.
	get	my hair	cut.

Noun clauses as objects

Tony **thinks (that)** a bullfight **will be** an exciting experience.
Gina **believes (that)** Spanish food **is** good for her diet.

Reported Speech

Commands

I would **tell** her **to be** supportive.
She **told** Lynn **to talk** to Lee.

Statements

Lee **said** (that) I **lived** near him.
She **said** (that) people **were talking** about us.
Gina **asked** Lynn **if** something **had happened** to her.
She **asked** Lynn **if** she **liked** the company.

COMMUNICATION SUMMARY

Talking about having/getting something done
Gina had her passport renewed.
She got her camera repaired.

Reporting opinions, thoughts, and feelings
Tony thinks that a bullfight will be an exciting experience.
Gina believes that Spanish food is good for her diet.

Reporting what other people asked or said
Gina asked Lynn if something had happened to her.
She said that people were talking about us.

Expressing advice
I would tell her to be supportive.

Reporting other people's opinions
My partner says he would never date someone at work.

Agreeing
I think that's a good idea.

Disagreeing
I can't say that I agree with you.

Complimenting
Your book is wonderful.